GRACE
// TRUTH
2.0

GRACE // TRUTH

2.0

Five More Conversations
Every Thoughtful Christian Should Have
About Faith, Sexuality & Gender

by DR. PRESTON SPRINKLE

THE CENTER FOR
FAITH, SEXUALITY & GENDER

Grace/Truth 2.0

© 2018 by The Center for Faith, Sexuality & Gender
All rights reserved.

No part of this book may be reproduced or transmitted in any form or by any means, electronic or mechanical, including photocopying, recording, or by any information storage and retrieval system, except for brief quotations in critical reviews or articles, without written permission from the publisher.

ISBN 978-0-9992072-8-4 (paper)
ISBN 978-0-9992072-9-1 (eBook)

Scripture quotations marked (ESV) are from *The Holy Bible, English Standard Version*®, copyright © 2001 by Crossway, a publishing ministry of Good News Publishers. Used by permission. All rights reserved.

Scripture quotations marked (NIrV) are taken from the Holy Bible, *New International Reader's Version*®, NIrV® Copyright © 1995, 1996, 1998, 2014 by Biblica, Inc.™ Used by permission of Zondervan. All rights reserved worldwide. www.zondervan.com The "NIrV" and "New International Reader's Version" are trademarks registered in the United States Patent and Trademark Office by Biblica, Inc.™

Scripture quotations marked (NLT) are taken from the *Holy Bible, New Living Translation*, copyright ©1996, 2004, 2007, 2013, 2015 by Tyndale House Foundation. Used by permission of Tyndale House Publishers, Inc., Carol Stream, Illinois 60188. All rights reserved.

Scripture quotations marked (NIV) are taken from The Holy Bible, *New International Version*®, *NIV*®. Copyright © 1973, 1978, 1984, 2011 by Biblica, Inc.™ Used by permission of Zondervan. All rights reserved worldwide. www.zondervan.com The "NIV" and "New International Version" are trademarks registered in the United States Patent and Trademark Office by Biblica, Inc.™

Cover Design by Jeff Gifford
Interior Design by Beth Shagene

Manufactured in the United States of America

18 19 20 21 22 23 • 19 18 17 16 15 14 13 12 11 10 9 8 7 6 5 4 3 2 1

Contents

Welcome! | 007

CONVERSATION 6: Us versus Us | 013

CONVERSATION 7: Shouldn't Christians Just Love Everyone? and Other Questions ... | 045

CONVERSATION 8: Sex, Gender, and the Bible | 079

CONVERSATION 9: A Grace/Truth Response to the Gender Conversation | 111

CONVERSATION 10: LGBT+ Inclusion in the Church | 143

Epilogue | 179

Welcome!

Welcome to part two of our *Grace/Truth* conversation on faith, sexuality, and gender! Most of you have already gone through *Grace/Truth 1.0*, but there might be some who are jumping in for the first time. To make sure we're all on the same page, let's sum up the main points in each of the five conversations in *1.0*:

1. LGBT+ questions are not just about issues; they're about real people with names and faces and stories. They're about Lesli, Joey, Jordan, Greg, Nate, Brad, Laurie, and other real people whom we met in our previous conversations. We shouldn't just debate Bible verses and politics without cultivating a lively compassion for people who are deeply affected by this topic.

2. Jesus embodies a *grace/truth* approach to people, especially people who were shamed and shunned by the religious elite. And many LGBT+ people have often been shamed and shunned by the Christian church. Jesus has a high view of truth, and he doesn't shrink back from calling people to repentance. But he also has a radical view of grace that extends love to those who have been rejected by religious people.

3. Christianity has always taught that marriage is between two sexually different persons—a man and a woman. A growing number of Christians have recently argued that marriage is between two consensual adults regardless of their sex difference. But the Bible says that marriage is the union between two sexually different persons, a position still held by most branches of global Christianity.

4. In both the Old Testament and the New Testament, the Bible explicitly prohibits same-sex sexual relations. Some people say these verses don't apply to modern-day consensual same-sex relations, but, as we demonstrated in *1.0*, these passages prohibit *all types* of same-sex relations—including consensual marriages.

5. There are several relational dos and don'ts that Christians can put into practice to embody Jesus' *grace/truth* way. We should listen and listen again, be a safe person for LGBT+ people to talk to, watch our posture so we don't send out wrong signals, focus on the gospel more than we focus on sexuality, not be afraid to say "I'm sorry," and make sure we're not hypocrites—always looking at the sin of others while ignoring our own.

If any of these sounds unfamiliar or you're not sure you agree with these points, then I encourage you to go back and read the relevant sections of *Grace/Truth 1.0* that correspond with each point (for example, number 1 above sums up conversation 1 in *Grace/Truth 1.0*, and so on).

In *Grace/Truth 2.0* we will do three things. First, we will take a deeper dive into the questions we wrestled with in part 1. For instance, we'll respond to some more complex arguments that affirming Christians make toward the traditional Christian view of marriage (see conversation 7). Second, we will address some questions that we didn't bring up in *Grace/Truth 1.0*, such as:

- *Can you truly love LGBT+ people while holding to a traditional theology of marriage?*

- *What does the Bible say about transgender people?*

- *Are some people born in the wrong body?*

- *How should Christians think about people born intersex?* (see conversations 8 and 9).

Third, our last section will take everything we've learned in *1.0* and *2.0* and apply it to ministry-related questions about membership, service, and leadership for LGBT+ people.

Remember: This book is part of a holistic learning experience. It's designed to be read in a five-week (or five-session) small group context. The format we envision is:

a) Each participant reads the relevant chapter (we call them "conversations") on their own before each meeting.

b) Then, as a group, you'll watch the video portion of that conversation when you meet together. The *Grace/Truth 2.0* videos are sold separately at centerforfaith.com, so make sure someone in your group has purchased them ahead of time (available in DVD or streaming).

c) After everyone watches the video, you'll talk through the questions at the end of each conversation. (If you want to be extra prepared, you should try thinking through the questions on your own before the meeting.)

For those who want to go deeper, please check out the optional podcasts and Pastoral Papers referenced throughout the book. Small group leaders can download our *Small Group Leaders Guide* for free under the RESOURCE page at www.centerforfaith.com.

If you're reading this book alone and you're *not* part of a small group, I would still encourage you to watch the videos related to each conversation and go through the questions by yourself. While it's designed for small group use, you'll still get a lot out of it going through it on your own.

And please note: There are ten conversations in all—five in *Grace/Truth 1.0,* and five in this volume, *Grace/Truth 2.0.* The five in the first volume are numbered 1–5, and the five in this volume are numbered 6–10.

A couple language reminders before we get started. First, I'll be using the acronym LGBT+ rather loosely to describe sexual and gender minorities regardless of their identity—that is, anyone who experiences same-sex attraction, gender dysphoria, or identifies as non-straight or non-cisgender. (Cisgender just means you're comfortable with your biological sex.) Second, when describing someone who believes that marriage is between a man and a woman, I'll primarily use the words *historically Christian* and sometimes *traditional* to describe this view. I no longer like the term *nonaffirming* to describe this view, since I think it can be misleading. I'll continue to use the word *affirming* to describe those who advocate for same-sex marriage in the church.

Let's get started with our first conversation!

CONVERSATION 6

Us versus Us

"Do you believe it's possible for Christians to truly love LGBT+ people and still believe in a traditional view of marriage?"

I asked my gay friend Drew Harper this question and was fascinated by his response. I'll tell you what he said in a second, but I want us to first linger on the question itself because it's such a vital one.

A number of Christians flat out say "no." They believe that you can't truly love and honor LGBT+ people without affirming same-sex marriage in the church. Some will even say that the traditional view of marriage and sexuality is harmful toward LGBT+ people. It causes gay teens to commit suicide and encourages the church to ostracize LGBT+ people. For instance, pastor and author Eugene Peterson publicly said that he believes in a historically Christian view of marriage, and one prominent affirming writer said that Peterson's belief will cause "Christian parents ... to force their LGBTQ children into conversion therapy" and will be used "to fracture relationships, to kick people out of churches and tell them God is disgusted by them"—all because one Christian pastor said that marriage is between a man and a woman.[1] For that affirming writer, a historically Christian view of marriage is intrinsically destructive.

Some say it's *not* possible for Christians to hold to a historically Christian view of marriage *and* truly love LGBT+ people. As we'll see, I believe this perspective is wrong. But don't take my word for it. Listen to the voices of LGBT+ people themselves.

The Untold Story of Religion and the LGBT+ Community

I've talked to many LGBT+ people who were raised in the church, and very few said they were harmed by the church's theology of marriage. Don't get me wrong. Many *were* harmed and harassed in the church, but not by theology. They were harmed by people. They were hurt by the silence, the shame, the isolation, the cold stares, the frightened expressions, the dehumanizing rhetoric. All the stuff we talked about in *Grace/Truth 1.0*.

Is all this shame and dehumanization a direct result of Christians believing that marriage is between a man and a woman? Does holding to a historically Christian view of *marriage* mean we must vilify LGBT+ *people*?

In 2016, a massive study surveying over 1,700 LGBT people[2] was released in a book titled *Us versus Us: The Untold Story of Religion and the LGBT Community*.[3] This book contains the largest scientific study on the religious background of LGBT people. According to this study:

- 83 percent of the LGBT community were raised in the Christian church.

- 51 percent of them left the church after they turned eighteen years old.[4]

I had figured many LGBT+ people had grown up in the church. Most of the ones I know have some sort of church background. But I didn't realize that the percentage was this high—83 percent! The fact that 51 percent of those who grew up in the church had left is, unfortunately, not that shocking. After hearing story after story about some pretty horrific experiences, it's no surprise that so many have left.

But then the study went on to ask the million-dollar question: *Why did you leave the church?*

Guess how many said that they left primarily because of the church's traditional theology of marriage?

Three percent.

Three percent of LGBT+ people who left the church said they left primarily over the church's traditional beliefs about marriage and sexuality. The perspective that a historically Christian view of marriage is driving LGBT+ people away is not shared by most LGBT+ people themselves.

Most of the other 97 percent who left talked about relational mistreatment, not harm caused by a doctrinal statement. Sure, some Christians misuse the Bible to justify their unkind behavior toward LGBT+ people. But we shouldn't blame the Bible or theology for this, any more than we should blame the U.S. Constitution when it's misused and abused. After all, LGBT+ people themselves talk about *relational* harm, not *theological* harm, in their past church experiences. Many, for instance, said they did not "feel safe," or they experienced a "relational disconnect with leaders," or they encountered an "unwillingness to dialogue," especially about sexuality. Or in some cases, they didn't leave the church; rather, the church left them—they were simply "kicked out" after it was discovered that they were gay.[5] In their own words:

> My problem isn't with God, it has always been with the institution that allows those who claim to obey God and yet make me feel most alienated (Sally, a 34-year-old lesbian raised in the church).[6]

Just to be clear, there's nothing intrinsic to a historically Christian view of marriage that should compel straight Christians to alienate gay people.

A lesbian named Tasha who was interviewed in the study said:

> All I wanted was to feel loved by those in the church I grew up with.... Love is giving me time to be with you to figure this out together. If you let any church people read this, tell them that I don't have to be right to feel loved. I have to be dignified in our disagreement (Tasha, a 21-year-old lesbian raised in the church).[7]

In testimony after testimony and interview after interview, LGBT+ people themselves describe their bad experiences in *relational* terms, not theological terms. They were unloved, mistreated, dehumanized, or isolated. As I said above, some *do* say that theology is what drove them away, but it's a very small percentage.

So what did my friend Drew Harper say when I asked him, "Do you believe it's possible for Christians to truly love LGBT+ people and still believe in a traditional view of marriage?"

I'll never forget how quickly and passionately he responded:

> I 100 percent believe that Christians can love and honor LGBT people—*truly* love and honor LGBT people—without changing their theology about sexuality.

As you'll see in the video portion of this conversation, Drew can say this so confidently because he's seen his parents do this very thing—*truly* love and care for LGBT+ people without changing their theology.

The problem isn't *what* we believe, but *how* we believe it—and I'm referring specifically to the times we hold to a right belief but wrongly mistreat people who live or believe differently.

If you want to love LGBT+ people well, then despite what you may hear in some popular media and from a vocal segment of affirming Christians, you don't need to change your theology of marriage. You need to embody the *grace/truth* way of Jesus: uphold a biblical sexual ethic (truth) while radically loving those who fall short of it (grace).

I know that for some of you, perhaps many of you, these questions really hit home. You have a son, daughter, sibling, father, friend, coworker, or neighbor who's gay or transgender. Or you're deeply concerned with injustices committed against the marginalized and oppressed, or you're sick and tired of seeing the church become a place of exclusion rather than inclusion. I want you to know that I'm right there with you. My heart aches for anyone—gay or straight—who hasn't experienced the scandalous welcome of Christ which says: *We want you here!*

The historically Christian view of marriage isn't the problem. The problem isn't *what* we believe but *how* we believe it—and I'm referring specifically to the times we hold to a right belief but wrongly mistreat people who live or believe differently. There is nothing within the traditional Christian theology of marriage that denies anyone the fundamental right to be human—to *flourish as full reflections of God's glorious image*.

Whoa, that last phrase may need more explanation! Whenever I teach on this topic and say things like this, it's inevitable that hands in the crowd shoot up with all kinds of questions. There's a good chance some mental hands sprang up in your own head when you read the previous paragraph. Let's wrestle with two of the top questions often raised at this point:

1. If some people are born gay, then isn't it unjust to tell them to *not* be who they are?

2. Can humans really "flourish as full reflections of God's glorious image" without getting married and having sex?

Then let's look at the vital role that singleness and spiritual kinship play in helping others flourish in the church. Finally, we'll circle back around to the statistics above and draw out some practical reflections on what these stats mean for the church today.

Are Some People Born Gay?

Some believe that gay people are "born that way" and therefore should be allowed to express their love in the context of a monogamous marriage. After all, they say, it's how God created them and God doesn't make mistakes.

Two things to consider. First, the Bible never says that if a desire feels innate and unalterable that it's therefore okay to act on. There's nothing in a Christian worldview that says really strong desires are part of who we were created to be and therefore should be acted upon. Quite the opposite. We are told that "the heart is deceitful above all things" (Jer. 17:9 NIV) and to resist the "cravings of our flesh and following its desires and thoughts" (Eph. 2:3 NIV). According to one of his college students, Richard Mouw sometimes said in class, "Whether you're gay or straight, we've all been made crooked by the Fall." We've been called to a crucified life of denying ourselves (Matt. 16:24) and resisting sexual desires and actions that don't align with God's will.

I love how Justin Lee, a gay affirming Christian leader, says it:

> Just because an attraction or drive is biological doesn't mean it's okay to act on.... We all have inborn tendencies to sin in any number of ways. If gay people's same-sex attractions were inborn,

> that wouldn't necessarily mean it's okay to act on them, and if we all agreed that gay sex is sinful, that wouldn't necessarily mean that same-sex attractions aren't inborn. "Is it a sin?" and "Does it have biological roots?" are two completely separate questions.[8]

So even if same-sex desires could be traced back to our birth, we are all born into a fallen world which affects our desires.

Plus—are people actually "born gay"? Is sexual orientation an innate, biologically determined by-product of God's design? Some people say "Yes, it's all due to *nature*!" while others say "No, it's all due to *nurture*!" (in other words, to the way people were raised). Both extremes are wrong, however. Most scientists say one's sexual orientation is caused by a complex blend of nature (biology) and nurture (environmental influences). According to the American Psychological Association (APA):

> [N]o findings have emerged that permit scientists to conclude that sexual orientation is determined by any particular factor or factors. Many think that nature and nurture both play complex roles.[9]

Please note: The APA *does* say that biology (or nature) plays a role—and sometimes a very significant one—in shaping one's orientation. To be very clear: Gay people don't choose their attractions any more than straight people choose theirs. In any case, what the science says is that sexual orientation can't be completely reduced to nature—a simple by-product of biology (or divine creation) with no environmental influence. Rather, both nature and nurture play complex roles and the nature/nurture dynamic differs from person to person.

And despite what you may have heard, *most* scientists agree. For instance, feminist psychologist Lisa Diamond considers the strict "born that way" theory to be an older, outdated, and disproven scientific theory.[10] Sari van Anders, a professor of psychology and women's studies at the University of Michigan, says: "The science of whether sexual orientation is biological is pretty sparse and full of disparate, mixed and replicated findings."[11] A massive survey was recently performed by Dr. Lawrence S. Mayer, a renown epidemiologist trained in psychiatry, and Dr. Paul R. McHugh, a distinguished professor of psychiatry at the Johns Hopkins School of Medicine. After examining more than 150 scientific studies that examined the cause of same-sex orientation, they conclude: "There are no compelling causal biological explanations for human sexual orientation…. The idea that people are 'born that way' … is not supported by scientific evidence."[12]

Again, just because something isn't 100 percent biologically determined *doesn't* therefore mean it's a choice. I wasn't born speaking English, and yet I didn't wake up one day and choose to be an English speaker. It sure feels innate, and I can't *not* speak English. But this doesn't mean I was created by God in the womb *as* an English speaker. I wasn't "born that way."

Can Humans Really Flourish Without Getting Married?

"I can live without sex," one of my gay friends tells me. "But I can't live without love and intimacy." I've been swishing this statement around in my brain ever since I heard it. There's a difference between love and sex, sometimes a massive one. Until we recognize and believe this, we will be tremendously unsatisfied.

Most Christians today focus unduly on marriage and family. Sometimes that focus reaches the point of idolatry—putting a life-expectation ahead of God and feeling tremendously unsatisfied if you never attain it. Most of us view singleness as an interim stage to get through, like standing in line for a ride at Disneyland. No one wants to be there, but we must grin and bear it so we can jump on a rocket and swirl around Space Mountain. Singleness is rarely viewed in a positive light in American Christianity. And this view runs counter to a biblical view of marriage, sex, and singleness.

The Old Testament does seem to elevate marriage and family. Some of this was for cultural reasons. In an agrarian society, it was tough to run the farm without a wife and kids and grandkids. This is why widows, orphans, and people who were childless had a hard time getting by, so God set up laws to help ensure that all people would be cared for. The ideal was to get married, have lots of kids, and die a happy man or woman with all your blood relatives around you.

But something changes in the New Testament—marriage and family become decentralized as a pathway for human flourishing. To be clear: marriage does not get *devalued* and it certainly doesn't get *redefined*. But the New Testament clearly *decentralizes* marriage as a prerequisite for flourishing and happiness.

Jesus said that your spiritual family is just as much family as your blood relatives (see Matt. 12:47–50). In some places, he seemed to *downplay* one's blood family compared with belonging to a family of believers. Paul clearly preferred the single life: "He who marries his betrothed does well, and he who refrains from marriage *will do even better*" (1 Cor. 7:38 ESV). While he didn't say it was wrong to marry, he said that singleness positioned you better for serving others, which Paul believed was the truest source of human joy.

Marriage and sex don't guarantee human flourishing. Only Christ does. And Christ perfectly embodied God's vision for flourishing *without* getting married and having sex.

I'm not sure that the modern church actually believes this. I think we subtly—and sometimes not so subtly—belittle people who aren't married, especially those who are of marital age. Think about the phrases we use. We see a beautiful thirty-five-year-old woman and we whisper to our friends, "Wow, she's so pretty. How come she's not *married yet*?" (As if all the pretty girls are destined to marriage, while all the ... what?... *ugly* girls are destined for singlehood?) Or: "Don't worry, God must have someone really special for you, since you've waited so long." (What if they die single? Did they not wait long enough? Did God forget about them?) Or: "Become the right person and you'll attract the right person." (Does this mean all single people haven't become the right person?)

Many of my celibate gay friends tell me that being single in the church is often harder than being gay in the church. They say it's not because singleness is so bad. It's because the church's culture is so rigidly focused on marriage and family that they don't feel like they belong as a single person. We may not say it outright, but we make single people *feel* inadequate, less important, or not living according to their fullest potential. And we do that even though, biblically, single people *fully* reflect God's image and can flourish as humans (as Christ did) without ever getting married.

The fact is, marriage is a small blip in our eternal life. We're all born single and called to steward our singleness for the first twenty or thirty or more years of our life. Most of us will be called out of singleness and into marriage and then called to steward our marriage to the glory of God. But most married people will be single again, whether through divorce or death of a spouse, and then we'll spend eternity with the family of God *as single persons once again* (Matt 22:30).

I hope you don't think I'm ripping on marriage and making singleness sound all peaches and cream. Both states bring their own blend of trials and temptations, suffering and joy, pain and comfort. LGBT+ Christians pursuing faithfulness have the added difficulty of not just being single but of also not having the prospect of ever dating, falling in love, and marrying a person they're attracted to. (Some do end up finding such love in opposite-sex marriages, but these success stories are rare.) LGBT+ Christians face real difficulties, and straight married Christian people like me need to empathize with our friends living such lives of celibacy. And our empathy must acknowledge the fact that human flourishing is not conditioned upon falling in love, getting married, and having lots of sex.

Discipleship is incredibly difficult, yes. Yet it's rooted in the hope that our earthly sufferings pale in comparison to the glorious reward of resurrection (Rom. 8:18).

Spiritual Kinship—the Key to Human Flourishing

Singleness shouldn't be equated with being alone, especially in light of what the New Testament says about the concept of spiritual kinship. Spiritual kinship refers to the rich, intimate, committed relationships that should be part of the fabric of belonging to a church. Spiritual kinship is the truest form of family envisioned in the New Testament.

In Mark 10, a rich young ruler asks Jesus about entering the kingdom of heaven, and Jesus tells him: "Go, sell everything you have and give to the poor, and you will have treasure in heaven. Then come, follow me" (10:21 NIV). The man went away sad, because the demand seemed too hard. But Peter proudly pats himself on the back: "We have left everything to follow you!" (10:28 NIV). To which Jesus responds:

> "Truly I tell you," Jesus replied, "no one who has left home or brothers or sisters or mother or father or children or fields for me and the gospel will fail to receive a hundred times as much **in this present age**: homes, brothers, sisters, mothers, children and fields—along with persecutions—and in the age to come eternal life." (Mark 10:29–30 NIV, emphasis added)

Sometimes we focus too much on the last part of the reward, "in the age to come eternal life." But Jesus says we receive a massive reward *"in this present age,"* namely: "homes, brothers, sisters, mothers, children and fields." Jesus isn't referring to getting married and owning a home, or having literal brothers and sisters and mothers. He's talking about the rich reward of receiving a spiritual family when you join the community of believers.

Spiritual kinship is one of the rewards Jesus gives us when we give it all up to follow him. It's fascinating that the New Testament is replete with commands to bear one another's burdens, pray for one another, encourage one another, and more than fifty other "one anothers." And almost none of these occur within the context of marriage. "Whoever does the will of my Father in heaven," Jesus says, "is my brother and sister and mother" (Matt 12:50 NIV).

Giving up the prospect of getting married doesn't mean giving up the possibility of love, intimacy, and *family*.

But here's the kicker. Most LGBT+ Christians don't experience the vibrant family envisioned by Jesus in the contemporary church. We've gotten good at telling gay people no to same-sex marriage and no to sexual relationships. But what are we saying yes to? *How are we embodying the reward of homes, brothers, sisters, mothers, children, and fields* that Jesus promises them? A sexual ethic that simply says no is an implausible ethic. It doesn't reflect the good news of the gospel—the "abundant life" that Jesus came to give us (John 10:10).

Ed Shaw is a celibate same-sex-attracted Christian, and he says that "the plausibility of the life that I have chosen is closely tied to" his experience with his spiritual family:

> When church feels like a family, I can cope with not ever having my own partner and children. When it hasn't worked is when I have struggled the most. The same-sex attracted Christians I've met who are suffering most are those in churches that haven't

grasped this at all and that don't even notice these individuals.[13]

If the church simply says no to sex and fails to say yes to becoming a spiritual family, then we're only doing half of what we're called to do. Let's follow Jesus all the way and become the reward Jesus wants his followers to enjoy.

Part of the roadblock to including LGBT+ people into God's spiritual family has to do with their lose-lose relational situation. Specifically, men (gay or straight) are told never to be alone with a woman. Gay people are also told (or it's strongly implied) that they shouldn't be alone with a person of the same sex. Well, who the heck are they supposed to hang out with, then? It gets really messy and absurd when you think about it. We straight folk need to realize that just because you're gay doesn't mean you're attracted to *everyone* of the same sex (including you). And just because two gay women are hanging out in a coffee shop doesn't mean they are inevitably going to wind up in bed together before the day's over. I think we need to chill out a bit over these relational dynamics and prioritize the deep need for relational connection, especially for LGBT+ Christians trying to live faithfully for Jesus.

Let's get super practical. What does spiritual kinship look like on the ground? Here are five suggestions that you can immediately put into practice.

One, watch your language and expectations. If you have kids, don't talk about their future as if it must include a spouse. If you're a leader or teacher, don't always use parenting illustrations in your teaching. When you're talking to others, don't assume they are married, will be married or even want be married someday.

Two, if you have a family, invite single people into it. Not just over for a quick meal, but invite them into family events like attending your kid's soccer game, or Sunday night "family nights" with pizza and a movie, or Saturday afternoon picnics. In other words, take Jesus' words about spiritual kinship seriously. Look, I've got a wife and four kids, and with the busyness of life, I understand how tough it can be to carve out time for your blood family, let alone including others into your precious family time. But I've found that when we invite others into our family, those are often the richest, most joy-filled moments of family time we experience. Quality, Christ-shaped family time looks outward, not just inward; it's inclusive, not exclusive.

Three, be particularly aware of how single people might feel on Mother's Day, Father's Day, or on any major holiday when people gather as families. Thanksgiving, Christmas, Fourth of July—whatever the occasion, take special note of any single people in your church who might be dreading certain days that have been deemed "family only" days, and invite them in.

Fourth, don't feel like you need to get all pro-gay around the LGBT+ people you're trying to relate to. You don't need to talk about how you have lots of gay friends or have never been creeped out at gay people. If something like this comes up naturally in the conversation, that's fine. But don't awkwardly interject proof that you're not homophobic. (Some of my black friends say that it's really funny how some white people feel the need to talk about how they love Martin Luther King, Obama, and hip-hop music when they're trying to relate to them.) Just be yourself and relate to people as one human to another.

Fifth, show the same physical affection toward LGBT+ that you would toward any human. Don't assume that if you hug a gay person of the same sex that they'll fall madly in love with you. Give a hug to whatever human might need a hug, and shake the hand of others who might be uncomfortable with a hug. The key is: *Don't treat LGBT+ people as special projects.* One of my celibate gay friends tells me, "We don't want to feel 'special-project-y,' so please don't think of it as: 'Hey, let's invite those lonely singles to lots of special church events, because Lord knows they need to be reached out to by you married people who have it together." Same thing with physical affection. We should include and not exclude, but don't be weird in *how* you go about including. Don't be awkward about giving hugs to all the gay people in your church while shaking hands with all the straight people. Just show appropriate physical affection to *people*—especially your spiritual kin. That's the main point. Single people are just as much part of the family as everyone else.

A Window of Grace

In the statistics I shared at the beginning of this conversation, 83 percent of LGBT+ people grew up in the church and 51 percent left after eighteen, and they left primarily for relational not theological reasons. As I linger on these stats, a question keeps popping into my head: How are we caring for the ones *who haven't yet left*?

The stats I quoted are not just helpful for understanding the past—those who *already* left the church—but crucial for understanding the present: those who have not yet left. If you do the math, there are millions of people in our churches who are LGBT+ or wrestling with their sexuality or gender identity on some level. They are in our youth groups, in our worship teams, in our leadership, and in our pews. Some are open about their struggles, but many are not. They are young, they are old, they are single, they are married to someone of the opposite sex. They are not just *they*. They are Mary and Tom and Gene and Stephanie and Steve. They are *us*.

How are they—or *we*—experiencing the love of Christ during the window of time while they are still at church? Statistically, if they don't experience it, many will leave.

When my friend Colin was in his early thirties (he's currently fifty-two), he was serving as a worship leader at a conservative church. He had realized he was gay during his teenage years but had kept it a secret from his church. While serving as a worship leader, Colin had fallen into an ongoing sexual relationship with another man. He would lead worship on Sundays and then hang out with his boyfriend throughout the week. This continued for several months until he felt convicted, broke off the relationship, and decided to confess his sin to the church. Remember—no one knew he even experienced same-sex attraction.

One Sunday night, he confessed his sin from the stage to a few hundred conservative Christians. And remember, this was more than two decades ago! How do you think that went?

They not only forgave him on the spot, but they received him with open arms of love. In fact, Colin told me that people were lining up to talk to him at the end of the service and were confessing their own sins to him. Apparently, Colin's courage to confess his sin gave them courage to come clean with theirs.

Colin experienced the radical love and forgiveness of God that day, but he didn't just receive it from God. He received it from God's people. And he received the reward of brothers and sisters, homes and mothers and fields that day and for many days forward. Colin has never left the church. He went on to get a degree in counseling and currently serves as a discipleship and family pastor at another large conservative Baptist church.

We hear a lot of negative stories about the experiences of LGBT+ people in the church. And we need to hear these stories in order to repent from our lack of grace. But we also need to hear success stories like Colin's to know that it can be done. It has been done. Indeed—it *has to be* done.

Let us press on and become a place of healing and flourishing for *all* of God's beautiful children.

QUESTIONS FOR DISCUSSION

1. What was your initial reaction to the question that started this chapter: "Do you believe it's possible for Christians to truly love LGBT+ people and still believe in a traditional view of marriage?" Did your response change as you read the rest of the chapter?

2. What is your response to the data that only 3 percent of LGBT+ people who left the church said they did so because of the church's beliefs on marriage and sexuality?

3. What was your reaction to the statistic that 83 percent of LGBT+ people were raised in the Christian church? In your own experience, do you find that LGBT+ people have a church background? Have they told you why they left?

4. Were you surprised when you read in this chapter that most modern scientists who have studied sexual orientation cannot say there is scientific evidence people are simply born gay? Do you feel that the average person on the street knows this? Or what is the common belief you hear about the cause of "being gay" from your friends?

5. Tasha said, "All I wanted was to feel loved by those in the church I grew up with.... Love is giving me time to be with you to figure this out together. If you let any church people read this, tell them that I don't have to be right to feel loved. I have to be dignified in our disagreement." Are you aware of ways you or others in the church leave LGBT+ people feeling unloved and undignified, as opposed to giving them "time to be with you to figure this out together"? List the ways, and suggest alternatives.

6. This chapter makes the case that "If you want to love LGBT+ people well, then despite what you may hear in some popular media and from a vocal segment of affirming Christians, you don't need to change your theology of marriage." But does that feel true to you, in practical terms? Do you know Christians, perhaps in your own church, who have a conservative theology of marriage and who would struggle to love LGBT+ people? Is there anything that would make that job easier for them?

7. Do you agree that people can truly flourish as humans regardless of sex and marriage? Why, or why not?

8. If you're married and you don't mind sharing, would you say that marriage has brought its own challenges to your life? What are some of those challenges, and what are some expectations you thought would be met in marriage that haven't been?

9. Brainstorm ways your church could "signal" to LGBT+ people that they would be safe in coming out, or for people with LGBT+ family members to admit that without shame. How might you bring up some of those ideas at your church?

10. What surprises you, if anything, about the story of Colin related at the end of this conversation? Could you imagine that reaction happening in your church? If not, how do you think your church *would* respond?

ENDNOTES

1 http://time.com/4859620/eugene-peterson-bible-homosexuality-gay-marriage.

2 Although I've used the acronym "LGBT+" in most places in the book, I've used "LGBT" here because that was the acronym used in the study cited.

3 Andrew Marin, *Us versus Us: The Untold Story of Religion and the LGBT Community* (Colorado Springs: NavPress, 2016).

4 The original statistic in Marin's study is 86 percent who were raised in *religious* communities, and this included both Jewish and Islamic communities, which comprised 2.7 percent of the LGBT people surveyed. I've therefore adjusted the percentage to 83 percent, which were raised in Christian (Catholic or Protestant) communities. Marin also says that more than 75 percent of all the people surveyed were raised in theologically conservative religious environments (ibid., 6).

5 See ibid., 31–63, for the various reasons and percentages for why LGBT people have left the church.

6 Ibid., 35.

7 Ibid., 83.

8 Justin Lee, *Torn: Rescuing the Gospel from the Gays-vs.-Christians Debate* (New York: Jericho Books, 2012), 62.

9 http://www.apa.org/topics/lgbt/orientation.aspx.

10 Lisa Diamond, *Sexual Fluidity: Understanding Women's Love and Desire* (Cambridge, Mass.: Harvard University Press, 2008), see 19–34, 71, 74, 228–29, 231, 235–37, 239–40.

11 https://www.usatoday.com/story/news/2017/06/16/born-way-many-lgbt-community-its-way-more-complex/395035001.

12 http://www.thenewatlantis.com/publications/number-50-fall-2016, 7.

13 Ed Shaw, *Same-Sex Attraction and the Church: The Surprising Plausibility of the Celibate Life* (Downers Grove, IL: IVP, 2015), 48.

CONVERSATION 7

Shouldn't Christians Just Love Everyone? and Other Questions ...

In *Grace/Truth 1.0*, we addressed some biblical arguments that affirming Christians have used to say that same-sex marriage should be celebrated in the church. In this conversation, we're going to wrestle with other questions that often come up. This will clear the way for us to discuss some gender- and transgender-related questions in conversation 8 and 9 before we navigate questions related to church membership, service, and leadership for LGBT+ people in conversation 10.

The questions we'll consider in this conversation are:

1. Shouldn't Christians just love everyone?

2. Doesn't the Bible give an ethical trajectory toward accepting same-sex marriages?

3. The Bible is super patriarchal; therefore, can it be trusted to teach us about marriage in the twenty-first century?

4. Haven't Christians been on the wrong side of history before?

5. If same-sex couples demonstrate the fruit of obedience, how can their relationship be wrong?

6. Since Jesus never mentions homosexuality, why do Christians make a big deal about it?

7. Isn't the historically Christian view of marriage harmful toward LGBT+ people?

Now, just a heads up. For most of this conversation, we're going to roll up our mental sleeves and engage some heady arguments. I'll try not to take us too deep—each argument could take an entire conversation. But I also don't want to dive too shallow. As faithful Christians, we really do need to hear, understand, and consider the reasons people give for holding to an affirming view.

> For a deeper look at these and several other affirming arguments, see our pastoral paper: "15 Affirming Arguments: And 15 Responses," available at centerforfaith.com/resources.

At the end of this meaty conversation, we'll come up for air and discuss a very practical point—one that is vital for relating to people who disagree with you on this issue. Or on any issue, for that matter. I don't want to spoil it, so stay tuned.

But first, let's strap on our thinking caps and get to work.

Arguments Used by Affirming Christians

1. Shouldn't Christians just love everyone?

This argument says that Jesus taught his followers to love people—all people—especially those who are marginalized. And it's unloving, they say, to deny people the right to pursue the romantic relationship they desire. After all, same-sex relationships aren't harming anyone, and why do Christians care about what two people do in the bedroom anyway?

Before wrestling with this argument, we must all check our hearts and ask: Have we been unloving toward gay people? Have you told a gay joke, laughed at a gay joke, looked down upon a gay person, or ignored someone who's wrestling with same-sex attraction or their gender identity? There are many ways in which straight Christians may have not been loving toward LGBT+

people. When we hear the "What about Love?" argument, we need to first repent from any unloving thing we've said or done.

As for the argument itself, it rightly prioritizes love but wrongly defines it. Jesus tells us to "love one another *as I have loved you*" (John 15:12 ESV), and that last part is important. When Jesus loved his disciples, he didn't always (or usually!) affirm their behavior or desires. It's worldly love, not Christian love, that says: *If you love me, you'll affirm everything I desire to do and everything I believe to be true about myself.*

Jesus-shaped (*agape*) love must be set alongside, not *against*, Scripture's sexual ethic. Jesus promoted an incredibly high ethical standard and yet scandalously loved those who fell short of it. And the direction of Jesus' love is always *toward* holiness, not away from it. This includes sexual holiness, scripturally defined. It's a false dichotomy to pit Christian love against Christian sexual ethics. Jesus promoted both.

Some people expand on the "just love everyone" argument by saying: "Do whatever you want as long as it doesn't hurt anyone." But this reasoning comes from secular humanism, not Christianity.[1] Christian ethics certainly *includes* not hurting others—"Love your neighbor as yourself" is the second greatest command.

Shouldn't Christians Just Love Everyone? and Other Questions ... | 049

But "Love the Lord your God with all your heart and with all your soul and with all your mind and with all your strength" (Mark 12:30 NIV) is the greatest command, and you can't seek to love God without trying to follow his design and direction for sexual holiness.

It's true, most sins end up hurting other people. But some don't. If I bow down to an idol in the secrecy of my basement, I'm not hurting anyone. If my wife and I didn't have kids, and we happened to "fall out of love with each other," we might not be hurting anybody by getting a divorce. But the Bible never reduces Christian obedience to "Do whatever you want as long as it doesn't hurt anyone."

True love of God and neighbor submits to God's will in every area of our lives—including human sexuality *and* how we treat LGBT+ people.

2. Doesn't the Bible give an ethical trajectory toward accepting same-sex marriages?

The trajectory argument agrees that the Old Testament condemns same-sex relations but insists that the New Testament begins to show signs of moving toward acceptance and affirmation. The New Testament doesn't come right out and say that same-sex marriage is okay. But we do see themes about loving our neighbor and accepting eunuchs and gentiles into the kingdom (Matt. 19; Acts 15). Therefore, we should follow this ethical trajectory that moves from rejection to acceptance and apply it to contemporary same-sex couples who are pursuing monogamy.

I agree that ethical trajectories exist. And if you've eaten bacon lately, so do you. Some things *prohibited* early on in Scripture are *permitted* later on (or vice versa). For instance, the Bible allows for slavery under Old Testament law, but we see clear signs that it's moving away from slavery when we get to the New. The Old Testament contains some demeaning statements toward women, but there's a trajectory moving toward the full equality of women in the New. And while the Old Testament condemns same-sex relations, there's a trajectory moving toward ...

Toward what? Do we actually see a trajectory moving toward including same-sex relations into a Christian vision for marriage and sex?

The fact is, not every command moves from prohibition to permission; many moral norms remain quite stable. No one would argue, for instance, that we should move beyond the Bible's concern for the poor and marginalized toward neglecting the poor and protecting the rich and powerful. Some commands and prohibitions remain the same from Genesis to Revelation.

In fact, some ethical trajectories get tighter, not looser. Take divorce, for example. If you follow the trajectory of divorce, the Old Testament is quite lenient, while the New Testament is much stricter. The same goes for adultery. Jesus actually tightens the reins when he says that lust is the same as sleeping with another man's wife (Matt. 5). When it comes to sexual ethics, there is a trajectory, but it moves toward greater strictness, not leniency.

From Genesis through Revelation, and continuing throughout church history (and much of human history), marriage as a union between sexually different persons—no matter how much divorce, adultery, lust, and other sins tear at its foundation—remains constant. That is, it remained constant until some Western churches in the late twentieth century redefined the meaning of marriage.

There is simply no evidence in Scripture that its view of marriage and sexuality is on a trajectory to include same-sex couples. Whenever same-sex behavior is mentioned, it's always prohibited. Whenever marriage is mentioned, sex difference is an essential part of it.

3. The Bible is super patriarchal; therefore, can it be trusted to teach us about marriage in the twenty-first century?

This argument overlaps a bit with the previous one. It's an attempt to recognize the biblical prohibitions and yet still get around them. The argument actually takes two directions. One has to do with the prohibition passages in the Old Testament (e.g., Lev. 18:22; 20:13) and the other has to do with a "biblical" view of marriage as a whole. Let's tackle the first one.

Some people say that in Old Testament times, men were more valued than women, and women were seen as little more than sexual receivers and baby makers. They conclude that the reason men were forbidden from having sex with other men is because in the act, one man must act "like a woman"—receiving rather than giving. In a patriarchal culture, where women were viewed as property and much less valuable than men, such an act would disgrace the superiority of men—the penetrators who should never be penetrated like a woman.

There's some truth to this argument. The Old Testament world was deeply misogynistic (i.e., it devalued women). But the Old Testament itself does not reflect this misogyny to the same degree.[2] Now, to be honest, there are some laws and statements that seem to uphold men as more valuable than women, but when considered against the backdrop of the rest of the ancient world, the Old Testament is quite liberating toward women. Several women are held up as heroes of the faith and more courageous than men (Rahab, Ruth, Deborah, Abigail, etc.). Plus, the creation account (Gen. 1–2) says that women equally possess the "image of God"—an exalted status claimed only by kings in the ancient world.

Because the Old Testament itself does not reflect the same degree of misogyny found in the ancient world, it's wrong to assume that the main problem God had with same-sex sex was that it turned the male "receiver" into a "mere woman."

Plus, there's nothing in the actual text of Scripture (in Leviticus or elsewhere) which supports this "patriarchal" argument. Read through Leviticus 18 and 20—there's nothing in the actual text which says that men shouldn't have sex with other men *because* this would treat another man as a lowly, baby-making, kitchen-bound woman. The commands in Leviticus simply state in absolute and unqualified terms: Men shouldn't have sex with other men. Affirming Christians who pump these commands full of patriarchal assumptions assume things about the text that are not clearly there.

> There is no such thing as a "biblical view of marriage" that we follow today. Back then, men were allowed to take multiple wives and concubines and to divorce their wives for all sorts of inhumane reasons.

Now, the second part of the patriarchal argument goes something like this: There is no such thing as a "biblical view of marriage" that we follow today. Back then, men were allowed to take multiple wives and concubines and to divorce their wives for all sorts of inhumane reasons. The Bible envisions only patriarchal marriages where men rule over woman with a heavy hand. Therefore, we actually shouldn't talk about a "biblical" view of marriage. Such marriages were oppressive toward women.

Some of what I said above applies to this argument—the Bible (especially the New Testament) actually views women much higher than this argument assumes. In any case, the traditional Christian view of marriage that I've been talking about in this study has to do only with sex difference in marriage, not all the cultural taboos that marriage in the ancient world endorsed. In other words, we need to distinguish between certain *cultural expressions of marriage* in the Bible (which may have been patriarchal) and the *intrinsic design of marriage* as between sexually different persons. As an ancient cultural expression, sure—many wives were expected to cook, and clean, and stay home to make babies. This may have been how many wives lived in that culture, but it is not part of the *intrinsic design* of marriage as expressed in passages like Genesis 2 and Matthew 19.

The Bible beautifully portrays marriage as a one-flesh union between two sexually different and *fully equal* image bearers. If the authority of Scripture means anything, this basic aspect of marriage shouldn't be tossed aside as a relic of Israel's patriarchal past.

4. Haven't Christians been on the wrong side of history before?

I often hear people argue that for hundreds of years, the church believed slavery was okay. We only recently realized that slavery is a horrible evil. Isn't the current debate about same-sex relations the same thing? Aren't Christians who believe in a historical view of marriage on the wrong side of history—much like our slave-owning ancestors?

It turns my stomach that so many confessing Christians actually held slaves, were blatantly racist, and viewed women as less valuable as men. But I don't think the analogy between slavery and a historical view of marriage is accurate or helpful.

Our current discussion is essentially about what marriage *is*, and about whether a Christian vision of marriage should include same-sex couples. It doesn't question the inherent value and worth of a human being, even though some will say it does. Let me say it loud and clear for the folks in the back: *LGBT+ people are beautiful image bearers of God and should be valued and honored as such!* Saying that God designed marriage to be a male/female relationship is not inherently degrading toward LGBT+ people. The slavery discussion, however, is all about whether some humans should be treated as property rather than God's image bearers. To compare the two is like comparing apples and astronauts.

Plus, let's look at the history of slavery and same-sex relations. For the last two thousand years, the church has always and unanimously viewed same-sex sexual relations as immoral—that is, until some branches of late twentieth-century Western Christianity deemed them to be sanctioned by God. But the same is not true of slavery. Throughout church history, various leaders opposed slavery. Leaders like William the Conqueror (1027–1087), Saint Wulfstan (1009–1095), Anselm (1033–1109), Pope Paul III (1468–1549), and even the great theologian Thomas Aquinas (1225–1274) opposed slavery, or at least certain aspects of it. Sociologist Rodney Stark says, "The problem wasn't that the leadership was silent. It was that almost nobody listened."[3] And this doesn't even include the fact that Christians led the way in ending slavery in the eighteenth and nineteenth centuries.

Christians are far from perfect; that's why we need a perfect Savior. But it's not as if the entire church for two thousand years was pro-slavery. The entire, global, multidenominational church, however, *has* held a uniform belief about same-sex relations until the late twentieth century in the West. It's one of the few things that global Christianity has agreed upon in the past two thousand years. Whether you're a miracle-working charismatic in Sao Paulo, an incense-swinging Russian Orthodox priest in St. Petersburg, or an Inuit pastor in northern Alaska—Christian leaders everywhere have held a uniform belief about marriage and same-sex relations. Christianity's variegated views on slavery have little in common with its globally uniform belief about same-sex relations.

It's true that Christianity has sometimes been on the wrong side of history and discovered later that it was indeed wrong. Belief in a flat earth comes to mind. But it also goes the other way. Sometimes Christianity has been on the right side of history while secular culture moved in an unhealthy direction. I mean, would anyone seriously argue that all advancements in society or scientific understanding always lead to moral progress? Certainly, the scientists behind genetically modified organisms (GMOs) or, more drastically, those who supported communist regimes in the late twentieth century thought they were on the right side of history—only to find out later that the old way was better.

The point is, whether something is moral or immoral needs to be evaluated based on its own merits, not just because it constitutes the majority opinion. Not every societal advancement is really an improvement on human flourishing. The question should be: *Is it true?* not *Is it new?*

5. Same-sex couples demonstrate the fruit of obedience. How can their relationship be wrong?

Gay couples can absolutely demonstrate many virtues in their relationship. They can be happy and kind and loving and generous and sacrificial and many other things that heterosexual couples strive to be. But some have used this fact as evidence that same-sex relationships therefore must not be sinful. After all, if such relationships produce virtuous fruit, then how can they be bad?

This is probably one of the most powerful *relational* arguments to wrestle with. It's easy to dismiss it logically. (And we'll address the logic of it below.) But relationally, it's tough to get to know a loving and kind gay couple, who might morally outshine your heterosexual Christian friends, and still conclude that same-sex relations must be bad. To be honest, if sexual ethics were solely determined by experience, then it would be really hard to say that *all* same-sex relationships are sin.

But sexual ethics must appeal to Scripture and Christian tradition. And when we look at Scripture (as we have done in *Grace/Truth 1.0*), we see that same-sex sexual relationships are not God's intention. If someone uses this argument to justify same-sex relationships, they must also provide a better interpretation of Scripture when it comes to marriage and sex.

The argument itself is tough to maintain with rational consistency. Just because a relationship might demonstrate some fruit doesn't mean the relationship itself is moral. A man and woman who are sleeping together outside the commitment of marriage could also give generously to the poor, donate their time at a homeless shelter, and be the most kind and humble people on earth. But none of these virtues justifies their sexual relationship.

The same goes for a same-sex sexual relationship. Whether their relationship is moral cannot be determined simply by looking at virtues that the couple exhibits. We can admire the virtues, learn from them, and even imitate them. We can believe that these two are incredibly good people and a gift to humanity. But a consistent and biblical sexual ethic cannot be determined by looking at the virtues of the couple alone. We have to look at Scripture to determine God's intention for sexual expression.

People who use the fruit-of-obedience argument often appeal to the fruit of the Spirit of Galatians 5:22–23 "love, joy, peace, patience, kindness," etc. If same-sex couples experience these things, then they must be filled with the Spirit and therefore their relationship is Spirit-filled. The problem, though, is that Paul contrasts the fruit of the Spirit with another list: the acts of the flesh, which includes "sexual immorality" (5:19)—a catch-all term that includes same-sex sexual relationships. Paul, the author of the fruit-of-the-Spirit passage, does not agree with the fruit-of-obedience argument.

6. Since Jesus never mentions homosexuality, why do Christians make a big deal about it?

It's true that Jesus never explicitly mentions homosexuality. Some people have understood this silence to mean he either doesn't care about it or he probably would have affirmed same-sex relations. But this is reading way too much into Jesus' silence. Here's why:

First, Jesus was a Jew, and first-century Judaism was the context of his life and teaching. The topics he debated with other Jews were always ones that were disputed within Judaism (like divorce or how to keep the Sabbath). But same-sex relations were never disputed within Judaism. Every Jew in Jesus' day believed that same-sex relations were against God's will—no scholar disputes this. And this is probably why Jesus never mentions it. It was a nonissue.

Second, Jesus *does* mention sexual immorality, for example, in Matthew 15:19 where he says, "For out of the heart come evil thoughts—murder, adultery, *sexual immorality* [Greek: *porneia*], theft, false testimony, slander." Again, every Jew in Jesus' day considered same-sex relations to be

> For an in-depth look at why Jesus never mentioned homosexuality, see our pastoral paper: "Why Didn't Jesus' Mention Homosexuality?" available at centerforfaith.com/resources.

sexually immoral based on the sexual laws in Leviticus 18. Even though Jesus doesn't directly mention same-sex relations, he does speak of them indirectly.

Third, as we mentioned above in our second argument ("Doesn't the Bible give an ethical trajectory toward accepting same-sex marriages?"), when Jesus disagrees with a traditional Jewish sexual ethic, he doesn't expand that ethic but tightens it. For instance, divorce was debated within Judaism. Some Jews were strict while other Jews were more lenient. When we look at Jesus' view of divorce, he held to a stricter view. Same with adultery. Many Jews believed that you haven't committed adultery unless you actually slept with another person's spouse. But Jesus tightens in the Jewish ethic: "But I say to you that everyone who looks at a woman with lustful intent has already committed adultery with her in his heart" (Matt. 5:28). When Jesus departs from a Jewish sexual ethic, he moves toward a stricter ethic, not a more lenient one.

Based on what Jesus does say about sexual ethics in general, there's no evidence that he would have affirmed same-sex relations if the question came up. Jesus' silence on homosexuality, therefore, cannot be taken as indifference or affirmation. We must interpret Jesus within his first-century Jewish context, not our twenty-first-century Western context.

7. The historically Christian view of marriage harms LGBT+ people

From my vantage point, this has become the most frequently used affirming argument. We briefly discussed it in the previous conversation, but given its popularity, it's worth revisiting to make sure we understand it.

Before we address this argument, we need to realize that the historically Christian view of marriage may feel like hopelessness to LGBT+ people. Discipleship doesn't harm us, but it is costly and even painful sometimes. This is why we cannot idolize marriage and sex as the only means of relational fulfillment. This is why we need to elevate spiritual kinship, singleness, and the confidence that this earthly life will not satisfy all our desires. Saying no to marriage without saying yes to kinship and intimacy *is* harmful to anyone trying to live in a way that's faithful to Jesus.

So, does this mean the historically Christian view of marriage *is* actually harmful? No, I don't believe it is.

As a preliminary point, the harm argument works only if the historically Christian view is untrue. If it's not from God, then yes, it could be incredibly harmful. But if it's from God, then it cannot be harmful. (Or if it is, then we have bigger things to worry about than same-sex relations!) God's words are painful at times. God's will isn't easy to follow and is sometimes tethered to a life of suffering. But joy and suffering aren't antithetical in God's eyes (Heb. 12:1–2). In short, difficulty isn't the same as harmful.

Now, as we saw in the last conversation, most LGBT+ people themselves don't believe that the traditional view of marriage is intrinsically harmful. Or in some cases, I'll hear people say they believe it is, but when I ask them to tell their story, they often end up talking about really bad *relational* experiences in the church. The idea that *theology* is the problem can become a quick category used to describe the real problem—relational trauma experienced in the church. Now, please don't assume that this is true in every case. Again, for some people, theology *is* their main problem with the church. And no one likes being told what they *really* believe. Don't assume you know their story better than they do. Instead, just listen to their story and let them tell you where the source of contention lies.

Since most LGBT+ people say that theology is not the main problem, where does this argument come from? Who are the ones saying that a historically Christian view of marriage is intrinsically harmful? Oddly enough, I typically hear this from *straight* (mostly white) affirming Christians and not from LGBT+ people.

I've got a friend who pastors a young, hip church in a very progressive city. He believes in a traditional theology of marriage, and around 10 percent of his church is LGBT+. Some are Christians, others are not. Some are affirming, others are not. *All* of them love the church and *none of them have left* when the pastor tells them—and he does tell them—what the church believes about marriage.

"Really?" I asked. "None of them get upset and leave when they hear that you hold to a historically Christian view?"

"Well, no *LGBT* people have left," he said. "But several straight, affirming Christians get very upset and leave the church when I tell them about my traditional views. *They* are the ones saying I'm a bigot and harming LGBT people, but none of the actual LGBT people at my church have said this."

I've found this to be true in many other churches I know. Many straight, affirming Christians are horrified at the traditional view of marriage, but LGBT+ people themselves are less likely to be turned off by it. They may disagree with it, or they may want to hear more. Either way, they typically don't stomp off in anger when they hear that a particular church believes what Christians globally have believed for two thousand years.

So, here are a few things to know about the harm argument:

First, according to the one study that has analyzed this question (i.e., Marin's study), most LGBT+ people themselves don't believe it.

Second, some Christians who believe in a traditional view of marriage *have* said things and done things that have harmed LGBT+ people. But this doesn't mean that a historically Christian view of marriage is itself intrinsically harmful. Biblical doctrines don't create bad people. Bad people misuse good doctrines to hurt people they don't like.

Third, it is true that ideas can influence people to do bad things. But there's nothing in the idea that marriage should be between two sexually different people that logically or psychologically should drive people to be unkind to LGBT+ people.

Now here's the thing. There *have* been people who have held to a historically Christian view of marriage and sexuality who have also done things that have really hurt LGBT+ people. Maybe some have even tried to justify their hatred of LGBT+ people by citing verses about same-sex sexual sin. This is an obvious misreading of Scripture, like citing verses against heterosexual sexual immorality and concluding that you must therefore hate straight people. If you came to that conclusion, and acted on it, you would be misusing a perfectly good and true portion of Scripture to discriminate against and hurt someone—which is exactly what we do when we use the biblical doctrine of male/female marriage to harm LGBT+ people.

Most importantly, the harm argument is typically used by someone who has experienced a lot of pain and trauma or has seen it in the lives of their friends, and we need to be sensitive to this. As Christians, we need to look beneath the arguments—especially ones that are irrational and inaccurate—and get to the heart of the one making the argument.

Logical Arguments Aren't the Real Issue

Here's the thing about *all* the arguments we've just been talking about—they're not the real issue. The main reason people hold to the affirming view is that they think it's the only way to truly love and honor LGBT+ people. The arguments we just discussed are important, but refuting these arguments rarely changes hearts. And the mind typically follows the heart. Or in the words of Jonathan Haidt: "Intuitions come first, strategic reasoning second."[4]

Dr. Jonathan Haidt is a world-renowned social psychologist who specializes in moral theory. Put simply, he looks at why people believe the things they do. After years of looking at why good people disagree on core moral and political issues, he learned that people typically believe certain things because they first *want* to believe them. In other words, *desire precedes belief.* Then, after believing it, they find rational reasons to support their belief. But the thing that anchors the belief is *not* primarily rational arguments. It's the desire to believe the thing in the first place.

If you've ever been in a heated argument with a loved one or spouse, you probably know what I'm talking about. You build rational argument upon rational argument, and your airtight, logically impeccable case is met with resistance. Then, perhaps, out of humility (or maybe just weariness), you stop arguing and begin listening to the person's heart. You seek to understand and you ask genuine questions. It's only then that their guard comes down and their kung fu grip on their perspective loosens. They may not change their view, but they're less reluctant to listen to yours.

I know. Because I'm typically the one with the kung fu grip, and my wife is the one who softens my heart with her grace.

What's driving the affirming perspective is a deep love and concern for LGBT+ people. I've never met an affirming Christian who doesn't have this type of love, but those same affirming Christians know that there are church environments that don't share this love. They've been around too many Christians who have been cold or dehumanizing toward LGBT+ people (their friends), or toward them.

Desire precedes belief. Intuition comes first, strategic reasoning second. If you want to have a profitable dialogue with loved ones in your life who hold to a different view of marriage, don't just exchange rational argument for rational argument. Sure, there's a place for rational arguments. But attacking the belief without getting to know the desire that's driving the belief will get you nowhere in a relationship. And quite frankly, until traditional Christians can truly love and honor LGBT+ people with that head-spinning kind of love that offends the religious today just as it did in Jesus' day, our arguments won't be heard anyway.

Until traditional Christians can show compassion and empathy toward LGBT+ people, our views won't carry much weight. They will feel cold and depersonalized—detached from the lives of real people. Compassion without truth is empty sentimentality; truth without compassion is lifeless and powerless in an age of justice. What we need is both. The gospel demands both. Faithful allegiance to God's design for human sexuality, *and* radical love extended to the marginalized.

Our truth will not be heard if our grace is not first felt. Because the greatest apologetic for truth is love.

QUESTIONS FOR DISCUSSION

1. How would you define Christian love? Cite passages in Scripture if you can think of them.

2. A popular phrase today is "Love is love." What people mean by this is that we should love people regardless of the ethical choices they make, and that disagreeing with someone's sexual ethic or sexual choices is unloving. How would you respond to the statement "Love is love"?

3. Have you thought about "ethical trajectories" in Scripture? Can you name any other things in Scripture that move from prohibition to permission (or vice versa)? (Example: killing your enemy in the Old Testament and loving them in the New.)

4. Do you agree that same-sex relations are always prohibited and do not exist along an ethical trajectory toward permission? Why, or why not? Do you know any passage in the New Testament which could suggest that Scripture is moving toward allowing same-sex marriage?

5. At an emotional level, do you tend to categorize sins in which someone is deliberately hurt—such as assault or robbery—as more serious than those in which no one (except perhaps the one committing the sin) is hurt, such as sex between consenting unmarried adults or a childless, amicable divorce? Why or why not?

6. Some people say that Ephesians 5:21–33 reflects a more patriarchal view of marriage where women are treated as less valuable than man. Please read this passage and discuss in your group whether this passage presents a low view of women.

7. Can you think of examples of marriages in the Bible—in either Testament, but particularly in the Old—that deviate notably from our Western ideals of marriage? In what ways?

8. Have you heard the "Christians are on the wrong side of history" argument before? How have you responded? How would you respond now?

9. Jesus never explicitly mentions homosexuality, but are there other things that Jesus says that are relevant for determining whether sex-difference is necessary for marriage? Where? And why is this important for our understanding of same-sex relations?

10. How would you respond to someone who says that a traditional view of marriage is intrinsically harmful?

11. Psychologists say that *desire often precedes belief.* That is, before someone believes something, before they can justify it, they usually *want* to believe it. Do you think that affirming Christians want to be affirming before they logically defend their stance? Would you say the same about Christians who believe in a historically Christian view of marriage?

ENDNOTES

1 The Humanist Manifesto of 1973 states: "While we do not approve of exploitative, denigrative forms of sexual expression, neither do we wish to prohibit, by law or social sanction, sexual behavior between consenting adults. The many varieties of sexual exploration should not in themselves be considered 'evil.'"

2 See Paul Copan's book *Is God a Moral Monster* (Grand Rapids: Baker, 2011). He does a great job looking at the seemingly harsh treatment of women in the Old Testament against the background of the ancient world.

3 http://www.christianitytoday.com/ct/2003/julyweb-only/7-14-53.0.html.

4 Jonathan Haidt, *The Righteous Mind: Why Good People Are Divided by Politics and Religion* (New York: Vintage, 2013), 106.

CONVERSATION 8

Sex, Gender, and the Bible

My friend Lesli was born a girl. But from the time she was four years old, she experienced life as a boy. She felt like a boy. Thought like a boy. Played like a boy. "When all of the other little girls wanted to play tea or house, I wanted to play football," Lesli told me. "At the age of four I proclaimed that Wonder Woman was going to be my wife and we would have superpowered children. I thought nothing of it." Lesli also remembers loving Jesus with all her heart from as early as she could remember.

> My earliest memories are of the church nursery and Sunday School. I have always known that I was a beloved child of God. I cannot remember a time when his truth was not an integral part of my life.[1]

Her struggle with her gender identity only increased when she got older, and this made it extra hard to fit in at her youth group.

> I started to keenly feel a distance between myself and other girls. I could not relate to their emerging womanhood. They were spending hours putting on makeup, styling their hair, and talking about boys. None of this interested me in the least.

Like most kids wrestling with their gender identity, Lesli was doing it alone. With no one to talk to, Lesli began to sink into dark periods of depression. And when isolation meets depression, suicidal thoughts quickly follow. "I lived this charade until high school rolled around," and it was then that "I was becoming increasingly despondent and suicidal."

Finally, wrestling with her faith and gender identity and wanting some spiritual guidance, Lesli went to her pastor to ask for help. "What did your pastor say?" I asked. "Well," she answered, "he escorted me out of the church and invited me never to come back again. And I didn't, for the next eighteen years."

In the midst of debates about bathroom laws and transgender persons in the military, the main question I want you to consider in this conversation is: *What kind of person will you be when God places a Lesli in your path?* What will you do to alleviate, not increase, her suicidal thoughts?

If all we do is treat the transgender conversation—or Lesli—as some issue to debate or a public policy to vote against, we will miss a beautiful gospel opportunity to embody the loving presence of Christ to someone in need.

People, not issues—that's our running theme. Let's keep that at the forefront of our minds as we dig into this rather complicated discussion.

Over the next two conversations, we're going to discuss a lot of things related to sex and gender. These two conversations belong together, but for the sake of space and time and to make them more manageable, we're going to split them. By all means, make sure you don't just read this conversation and skip the next one, or vice versa! You won't understand one without the other.

So, in this conversation (8), we're going to

- Learn the correct terminology
- Examine the difference between sex and gender

- Explore nonbinary gender identities
- Study what the Bible says about male and female
- Distinguish between cultural and biblical views of gender

That'll be more than enough to chew on for this conversation. In the next conversation (9), we'll engage some important science-related questions, discuss the significance of intersex persons, and then spell out four key relational takeaways from these two conversations.

Oh, and at the end of this conversation, we'll revisit Lesli's story. There's much more to her journey; you won't want to miss it! But let's unpack some important terms first. As always, we have to understand what the relevant words and phrases mean in order to have a meaningful conversation.

Learning the Correct Terminology

Transgender

Transgender is an umbrella term for the various ways in which some people experience incongruence between their biological sex and their gender identity.[2] In layperson's terms, a transgender person often feels like they're trapped in the wrong body.

Please note: Most transgender persons *don't* get a sex change (technically: sex reassignment surgery, or SRS) and/or cross hormone treatment (or CHT) to alter their biological sex. According to one survey, only 3 percent of transgender people pursue sex reassignment surgery, so don't equate *transgender* with someone who's had a sex change.[3] Also, when I use the term *transgender* or talk about people who are transgender, I'm only talking about the experience and/or identity of people. I'm not saying that a biological female *is actually* a male (or vice versa) if they identify as transgender. We'll dig into this in more detail below.

Transsexual

This term is similar to *transgender*, but it usually refers to someone who *has* had sex reassignment surgery and/or CHT, or is seriously considering doing so. However, hardly anyone who has transitioned prefers the term *transsexual*. It's kind of like the term *homosexual*—it's an older term used in science labs but not in real relationships. Typically, people prefer *transgender* over *transsexual*.

Gender Dysphoria

Gender dysphoria is a fairly new term used by psychologists to describe the level of distress that often (but not always) comes with being transgender. Many people who identify as transgender experience gender dysphoria, but some don't. And not everyone who experiences gender dysphoria identifies as transgender.

Intersex

An *intersex* person is someone who is born with some atypical features in their sexual anatomy and/or sex chromosomes. As we'll see in the next conversation, intersex persons don't constitute a "third sex" or something other than male or female.

Nonbinary Gender Identities

A *binary* is something that has only two options. Think of it as an either/or, black or white, good or bad, or—male *or* female. So, *nonbinary gender identities* refer to identities other than male or female. You may have heard of terms like *gender-queer, gender-fluid, pangender*, or *gender nonconforming*. These are all *nonbinary* identities; they are used by people who don't identify as exclusively male or female.

Confused yet? That's okay. This might be a lot to take in for some of you. For others, this is all pretty basic stuff you learned in your first year at college and might feel like a real yawner. Whether you feel like this is all old news, new news, or fake news, I want to encourage you to be sensitive to others who are coming to this material from very different places and backgrounds. What feels over your head might be simple for others. What feels basic to some might be super challenging to the rest. And, at the end of the day, we need to join with each other to become the hands and feet of Jesus when God puts a Lesli in our paths! The first step to doing that is understanding some foundational terms.

With that in mind, let's discuss two more terms more thoroughly: sex and gender. It's absolutely essential that we explore these terms carefully.

Sex and Gender: Is There a Difference?

The first one is easy: *sex* simply refers to one's biological sex, which is typically self-evident. More precisely, a person's sex is determined by their sexual anatomy, reproductive organs, endocrine systems (think: hormones), and chromosomes (men have XY chromosomes while women have XX).

Gender, however, is one of the most elastic, misused, and confused terms used today. Up until the 1970s, *sex* and *gender* were used synonymously: sex *was* gender and gender was sex. But in the last few decades, *gender* has been used to mean many different things. While there are more than a dozen different ways in which people understand the term *gender*, most people use it to mean one or more of the following:

> a) *Your own internal sense of self*
>
> b) *How you express yourself (clothing, mannerisms, interests, etc.)*
>
> c) *Cultural expectations for what it means to be a man or a woman*
>
> d) *One's biological sex*

As you can imagine, discussions can get muddled quickly when people are using the same word to mean different things. It's like that scene in *The Princess Bride* when Inigo Montoya says (in a Spanish accent): "You keep using that word. I do not think it means what you think it means." Likewise, people sometimes use the term *gender* without knowing exactly what they mean by the term, and this compounds the confusion.

If you're ever in a conversation with someone about gender, I would go no further until both of you define exactly what you mean by the word. If people aren't using the same word in the same way, dialogue is impossible.

Sex, Gender, and the Bible | 087

Understanding the different meanings of gender also helps us understand why Facebook, for instance, now lists 71 different gender options and Tumblr lists 117, including *agender*, *blurgender*, *demigender*, *genderblank*, and many others. This is where most people who grew up without social media throw up their arms at the apparent madness and declare—*there are only two genders!* And they're right—if by "gender" they mean biological sex.

You probably want to know what I think about all of this! Okay, here are my thoughts.

Put simply: "*Sex* is a bodily, biological reality, and *gender* is how we give social expression to that reality."[4] In other words, both sex and gender are binary—male and female are the only two options. Humans are male (sex), which is expressed in maleness (gender), or they are female (sex), which is expressed in femaleness (gender). Now, it's obviously true that people experience and express their masculinity or femininity in different ways, and some people experience intense gender dysphoria. But it's unhelpful to create a different gender identity for every individual experience, and it's unscientific to completely separate

> "*Sex* is a bodily, biological reality, and *gender* is how we give social expression to that reality."

the idea of gender from biological sex. Biology tells us that there two sexes, male and female, not an infinite spectrum with male and female at opposite ends.

I'm fine with using the term *gender* to describe the various ways people (a) conceive of themselves as male or female, or (b) the way they express themselves, or (c) the societal expectations of femininity and masculinity. The term gender might be a good word to describe how we present ourselves as male or female. But I'm using the term gender *within*, not *in addition to*, the two biological sexes of male and female.

(Please reread and chew on that last sentence if you need to. It's absolutely crucial, so we can't move on until we're tracking with each other.)

That is, males will express themselves and experience their maleness in many different ways, and females will do the same. But these diverse experiences should be understood *within* (not *in addition to*) the binary of male and female.

We'll look at what the Bible says about all of this in a minute. But first, let's see where this sex and gender discussion has led to today—especially with a younger generation.

Beyond He or She

In March 2017, *Time* magazine ran an article titled "Beyond He or She: The Changing Meaning of Sexuality and Gender." One of the things that the article highlights is the popularity of nonbinary identities among younger people. Either/or categories like male or female, or gay or straight, are quickly becoming old school among teens today.

The *Time* article cites a recent survey that asked respondents to write in a term that best fits their gender. They received more than five hundred unique responses. Another survey found that one-third of younger people identify as neither gay nor straight but somewhere in between. More than a thousand young people were asked about Facebook's many gender options, and at least one-third of them said that seventy-one was about right or *not enough*. One interviewee for the *Time* article was asked about the categories of gay and straight and said: "I totally believe there are a 100, 200 shades in the middle."

Even the identity *transgender* is becoming less popular, since it still assumes a binary—a transgender person typically identifies with a gender *opposite* from their biological sex, which assumes only two options. Younger people are more likely to identify as gender queer, gender fluid, or gender nonconforming than they are transgender. Even if they don't personally identify this way, as many as 50 percent of millennials believe that male or female *aren't* the only two options.[5]

I can't emphasize enough that all of this nonbinary stuff is the ideological reality for most younger people today. If you think this discussion is a waste of time or some insignificant rabbit trail, then it's going to be much harder for you to help navigate these discussions with people who feel right at home in the world of the in-between. So if you need another cup of coffee, then please do grab one and maybe toss in an extra shot of espresso. Understanding these concepts isn't everyone's cup of tea—or coffee—but we must be culturally aware if we're going to be gracefully effective.

Now, I'm a huge fan of respecting individuality. We are all unique individuals and experience life differently. But I think that slapping a different gender identity on every individual expression or experience is unhelpful and confusing. (And if we go this route, then we truly need an infinite number of gender identities since there are an infinite number of individual experiences and expressions.) Biblically, as we're about to see, humans bear God's image as male or female. Your internal sense of self, or how you

> I don't think God ever wanted humans to construct gender identities that are disconnected from our biological sex.

express yourself, or cultural expectations of gender, are all descriptions of *how* you are male or female, not additional identities *to* male and female. Put simply, I don't think God ever wanted humans to construct gender identities that are disconnected from our biological sex.

To understand how I've come to that conclusion, let's turn to the Scriptures.

What Does the Bible Say about Sex and Gender?

It's almost beyond dispute that the Bible presents humanity as a male/female binary. Here's a brief overview of what the Bible says.

First, the Bible only identifies two different sexes: male and female. We see this clearly in the creation account (Gen. 1–2), but also throughout the rest of Scripture. Consider what Genesis 1:27 says, and pay special attention to the relationship between male, female, and God's image:

> God created mankind **in his own image**,
> **in the image of God** he created them;
> **male and female** he created them.
> (Gen. 1:27 NIV, emphasis added)

Notice that "male and female" is correlated with the previous references to "the image of God" and "his own image." That is, our biological sex differences are part of what it means to reflect God's image. God's image is displayed *through* both males and females. God could have created an androgynous humankind to reflect his image, but there's something unique about female *and* male that conveys the diverse and beautiful aspects of God.

> For an in-depth look at what the Bible says about sex, gender, and transgender experiences—including all the pushbacks—see our pastoral paper: "What Does the Bible Say About Sex, Gender, and Transgender Experiences?" available at www.centerforfaith.com/resources.

Second, the Bible doesn't consider sex and gender to be two totally different aspects of humanity. Throughout the Bible, biological females are expected to identify as women, and biological males are expected to identify as men. People may experience their sense of gender in different ways. Some women are praised for having babies, while others are celebrated for winning wars. But there's nothing in the Bible that considers sex and gender as two totally different realities.

Part of this is because a Judeo-Christian view of human nature values the body more than many other philosophies or religions. According to Christianity (and Judaism), we don't just *have* bodies; we *are* bodies. Our bodies tell us who we are, even if our minds disagree. Yes, we have immaterial aspects of our human nature. But these are viewed as *part of* our embodied existence, not something separate from of it. We are not souls with bodies, but embodied souls.

So, we can't identify ourselves without referencing our body. Our bodies are part of the identity that God has assigned to us. God expects biological females to identify and live as women and biological males to identify and live as men. (As we'll see in the next conversation, however, the Bible is quite flexible on the *way* you live out your biological sex.) When some people experience incongruence between their internal sense of self and their bodies, a biblical worldview does not allow for one's internal sense of self, or one's gender identity, to overrule our bodily existence.

This might raise some scientific questions in your mind, like *doesn't science say that some people really are born into the wrong body or have a male brain and a female body?* Don't worry, we'll address these in the next conversation.

Third, Scripture consistently prohibits crossing gender boundaries—men presenting themselves as women, and vice versa. For instance, Scripture prohibits cross-dressing (Deut. 22:5), condemns men who fundamentally confused gender distinctions (1 Cor. 6:9),[6] upholds culturally appropriate expressions of gender difference (1 Cor. 11:14), and critiques cultic practices that blur gender distinctions (Deut. 23:17–18). In fact, 1 Corinthians 11:2–26 assumes that the male/female binary is part of God's created order.[7] And the biblical prohibitions against same-sex sexual relations, most notably in Romans 1:26–27, are rooted in God's creational design for humanity as two sexually different persons (cf. Lev. 18:22). To present yourself as the opposite sex goes against the way in which God desires his people to reflect his image.

In short, the Bible not only affirms and promotes an embodied existence as male or female, but it also prohibits identifying as the opposite sex.

Now, some argue that when Jesus spoke positively about eunuchs ("there are eunuchs who are *born that way*" [Matt. 19:12]), he affirmed nonbinary or gender nonconforming identities. But Jesus wasn't saying that eunuchs were some other sex or a different gender outside the male and female binary. In the ancient world, eunuchs were simply infertile men, or men who had some abnormality in their male genitalia (typically through castration).[8] Because of this, they were sometimes considered *by others* to be less manly and were mocked for lacking the ability (or equipment) to father a child. Now, it's definitely possible that as a result of societal shame, eunuchs developed what we now call gender dysphoria. But there's no evidence that Jesus was thinking about people who identified as the opposite sex, and he doesn't bring up eunuchs to challenge the male/female binary. In fact, he had just appealed to the male/female binary a few verses earlier (see Matt. 19:3), so it's unlikely that Jesus is going against what he just said.

Most importantly, though, notice that Jesus speaks positively about eunuchs. He never mocks or denigrates people who fall outside what the vast majority of us experience in being male or female, and he doesn't mention the eunuch as some ideological example to confront. Jesus acts very differently than some people do today who only mention, say, transgenderism as an ideology to attack and mock rather than as people to be loved. Sure, there are ideologies that need to be confronted and deconstructed, but not at the expense of loving people as Jesus loved them.

In short, Jesus doesn't talk about eunuchs in order to challenge the male/female binary. He brings up the eunuch to elevate singleness as a God-honoring vocation and to show that God's kingdom has a special place for those who have been "othered" by society.

From Genesis to Revelation, God intends humans to live out their gender identity in ways that are congruent with their biological sex. When people experience incongruence between their sex and gender, they (like all of us!) are experiencing the real effects of living in a fallen world where "things are not the way they're supposed to be."[9] And we simply *cannot* downplay, mock, or react coldly to the *very real experiences of those who suffer some sort of incongruence between their biological sex and their gender experience.* If you've never sat down and listened to the story of someone experiencing gender dysphoria and felt compassion for them as beautiful, image-bearing masterpieces, I would challenge you to do so. There's no substitute for entering into someone else's story.

Cultural versus Biblical Expectations of Gender

But this raises the question: What does it mean to live out your biological sex? That is, what does it mean to act like a man or a woman? Unfortunately, there's quite a bit of confusion over this question, both outside and inside the church. Put frankly, I think many Christians adhere more to cultural expectations of gender than to biblical ones.

Here's an example. Imagine it's Super Bowl Sunday. Your pastor, a man, gets up and tells the congregation something like this:

> *I hope you all enjoy the game this afternoon. Personally, I'm not going to watch it. I actually don't like football. It's way too violent; it saddens me when people physically hurt each other. Instead of watching the game, I'm going to attend a new musical that's playing downtown and then have dinner at a vegan restaurant next door.*

My guess is that the church would get pretty quiet. People would probably think he was joking, because, after all, real men love football, red meat, violence, and hate to watch musicals. At least, that's the cultural narrative we've been raised with.

But if we are Christians who believe in the Bible, our main question should be: Has your pastor broken any biblical expectation for real masculinity?

The answer is no. There's nothing in the Bible that says men must live like the good ol' boys of twenty-first-century America. The Bible never says that men must be athletic, unemotional, and aggressive. Think about it. Were Bezalel and Oholiab being manly men when

God gifted them to make "artistic designs" and sew "finely worked garments" (Ex. 31:1–10)? Or were they only masculine when they were "cutting stones" and "carving wood" (Ex. 31:4–5)? Was David being a man when he was killing Goliath, or when he was playing his harp and writing poetry? Was Deborah being feminine when she led Israel to war (Judges 4)? Was Jael living out her womanhood when she drove the tent peg through Sisera's head (Judges 4)? And how about that Proverbs 31 woman? Is she being feminine when she "considers a field and buys it" (31:16) or only when she "provides food for her family" (31:15)? Was Jesus being masculine when he cried over Jerusalem and said he wanted to gather his people as a mother hen gathers her chicks (Matt. 23:37)? Or was he only being manly when he turned over the tables in the temple (Matt. 21:12–17)?

If we stick to the Bible, the categories of masculinity and femininity—gender expression and experience—are very broad. (Again, this doesn't mean there are many different genders but many different ways of being male or female.) Many of our assumptions about masculinity and femininity come from culture, not Scripture.

Sorting out cultural versus biblical views of femininity and masculinity has practical implications. My friend Lance was a worship leader at a megachurch in California until he came out as gay and ended up leaving the church.

When he first told me his story, he mentioned in passing something I'll never forget.

"You know, Preston, I never doubted my masculinity until I started going to church."

Confused, I asked him to explain.

"Well, it was at church that I realized that men are supposed to drive muddy 4X4 trucks, love sports, and crave red meat. But I liked none of those things. I was actually into things like music, art, and fashion—but the church's view of masculinity felt like a small box that I was supposed to fit into. It was only then that I thought: maybe I'm not a *real* man."

After I heard that, I thought about all the men's retreats I've been to that reinforced cultural expectations of masculinity. People like Lance typically don't do well at these retreats since they color outside the lines of *cultural* masculinity, even if they've never crossed the boundaries of *biblical* masculinity.

We desperately need to teach biblical, not cultural, masculinity. To be sure, sex difference is very real. God created us as male or female. Our biology is different, and our psychology is different (though there are many similarities too).[10] But *biblical expectations for what it means to be a man or a woman are much broader than people realize.* And this might contribute to the current confusion over gender so prevalent in the church and culture today.

There's a lot more we could say about biblical expectations of gender roles, and much has been written on it. My main goal here is not to exhaust the topic but to start a conversation. What are the biblical requirements specific to being male or female? And what are some cultural assumptions that aren't necessarily in the Bible? Sorting out the biblical from the cultural might be the key that clarifies much of the confusion over sex and gender.

What Kind of Person Will You Be?

As you recall, Lesli was escorted out of the church after admitting that she struggled with her gender identity. She quickly found love and community with other LGBT+ people. She also fell in love with a woman named Sue, and they ended up getting married. Six years into their marriage, Sue contracted a rare disease that caused her hands to shake. One night, Sue went outside to light a cigarette and her hands were shaking so badly that she ended up lighting herself on fire. After being rushed to the hospital, the burns were so severe that she never recovered. Sue died in the hospital.

Lesli had already been through enough trauma throughout her life, and now this? The crushing blow of losing a spouse was more than she could handle. Half dazed, she scrambled to find a phone book to find a church that might do Sue's funeral. Lesli hadn't been to church in years, so she pressed her finger on the first number she found and dialed the phone. It happened to be a conservative Christian church, one of the most conservative churches in the area. The pastor happened to pick up the phone. Stammering, Lesli said: "Hi, my name is Lesli, and my wife just died. Um ... we're lesbians, but ... um ... I want to know if you would do my wife's funeral."

The pastor didn't say, "Let me think about that," or "Maybe, but you have to first know where we stand on the issue of homosexuality." With compassion and conviction, the pastor said:

"We would be *honored* to."

The pastor and the church surrounded Lesli with much-needed love—something she had never felt from Christians—and it was this simple embodiment of Christ-like love that reignited Lesli's passion for Jesus and brought her back to the faith.

Lesli is one of the most beautiful, Christ-like, sacrificial people I've ever met. She spends the bulk of her time now helping other people who are wrestling with their faith and gender identity. I've seen her stay up until the wee hours of the night, talking people down from suicide. She's an amazing gift, not an issue, to the church. She still wrestles with her gender identity, but now she has a loving church—her spiritual family!—to come alongside her in that struggle.

We've covered a lot of ground in this conversation, and your brain might be on information overload. It's necessary to be informed and to think through these things, but sifting through these ideas should never harden your heart toward people who genuinely struggle with their gender identity or feel marginalized because they don't look like everyone else.

As you continue to think through questions related to sex, gender, transgender, and nonbinary identities, just remember: *There might be a fourteen-year-old girl in your youth group on the verge of suicide because she doesn't feel like a girl and she has no one to talk to*. She was created in God's image and is beloved by Jesus. Will she be loved by the church? Will she be loved by *you*?

What kind of person will you be when God places a Lesli in your path?

QUESTIONS FOR DISCUSSION

1. What would you have liked to say to Lesli when she was a teenager wrestling with her faith and gender identity? How would you embody both grace and truth if she reached out to you for help?

2. Did this chapter clarify for you the differences between the meanings of the words *sex* and *gender?* Do you still have some lack of clarity about their meanings? In what way?

3. What do these sentences from this conversation mean to you: "We are not souls with bodies, but embodied souls. So, we can't identify ourselves without referencing our body. Our bodies are part of the identity that God has assigned to us." Discuss.

4. Do you know anyone who is transgender? Describe your relationship with that person and how you've tried to view them in light of the gospel.

5. Do you struggle with having empathy toward transgender people? Why, or why not?

6. Do you think that our culture's expectation of gender is different from Scripture's? That is, what does the Bible say about manhood and womanhood, and what does our culture teach us? Do they teach the same thing?

7. In what ways can the church make space for people who don't match up to gender stereotypes that come from culture but not the Bible? (For example: real men love sports; real women love to cook.)

8. If your son, daughter, or friend told you they are transgender and now want to be referred to by pronouns different from their biological sex, what would you say and why?

9. If you wouldn't mind sharing, have you ever felt like you haven't matched up to your culture's expectation of what it means to be a man or a woman? Please explain what that feels like.

10. If someone tells you, "Gender is a cultural construct," what do you think they mean by this, and how would you respond?

11. Do you think it would ever be okay for a Christian to get a sex change? Why, or why not?

ENDNOTES

1 Quotations attributed to Lesli are taken from personal communications from Lesli to the author.

2 According to Christian psychologist Mark Yarhouse, *transgender* is "an umbrella term for the many ways in which people might experience and/or present and express (or live out) their gender identities differently from people whose sense of gender identity is congruent with their biological sex" (*Understanding Gender Dysphoria: Navigating Transgender Issues in a Changing Culture* [Downers Grove, IL: IVP Academic, 2015], 20)

3 http://www.transchristians.org/book/book-objections/objection-sex-never-changes

4 Ryan T. Anderson, *When Harry Became Sally: Responding to the Transgender Moment* (New York: Encounter Books, 2018), 149.

5 https://fusiondotnet.files.wordpress.com/2015/02/fusion-poll-gender-spectrum.pdf

6 The Greek word Paul uses in 1 Cor 6:9 is *malakoi,* which refers to men who fundamentally confused gender distinctions. See Sprinkle, *People to Be Loved; Why Homosexuality Is Not just an Issue* (Grand Rapids: Zondervan, 2015), 106.

7 If you read 1 Corinthians 11, you'll see that Paul draws some *culturally specific* applications of male/female sex difference, such as the length of hair between men and women. The fact that Paul draws some culturally specific applications (i.e., these applications are not for every culture of every age) from the male/female distinctions doesn't mean that the very male/female distinction is *also* bound to that specific culture. The point is, Paul's entire discussion is predicated on the creational distinction between males and females, and that distinction is not limited to a specific culture.

8 See Edwin M. Yamauchi, "Eunuch" in *Dictionary of Daily Life in Biblical & Post-Biblical Antiquity*, vol. 2, ed. Edwin M. Yamauchi & Marvin R. Wilson (Peabody, MA: Hendrickson, 2016).

9 Cornelius Plantinga, *Not the Way It's Supposed to Be: A Breviary of Sin* (Grand Rapids: Eerdmans, 1996).

10 For psychological evidence of sex difference, see the highly acclaimed work of Harvard professor Dr. Steven Pinker, *The Blank Slate: The Modern Denial of Human Nature* (New York, NY: Penguin Books, 2003), esp. 337–71.

CONVERSATION 9

A Grace/Truth Response to the Gender Conversation

"Sure, the Bible says that biological males are males, and biological females are females," my friend told me. "But we now know from science that it's not so simple. Some people are born into the wrong body, so that they truly are the gender opposite from their biological sex."

What would you say to my friend? Does science really say that someone could have a female body but really be male (or vice versa)? And if so, should we modify what the Bible says in light of modern science? After all, some say, the Bible also talks about the sun rising upon the earth instead of the earth revolving around the sun. We've advanced in our scientific understanding of a heliocentric solar system, so haven't we also advanced in our knowledge of sex and gender? Plus, some people are born intersex—neither male nor female. Doesn't this show that male and female aren't the only two options?

In the first half of our conversation, we'll wrestle with what scientists have said about transgender and intersex persons. In the last half, we'll refocus our attention on how we can embody the grace and truth of Christ toward those who are wrestling with their gender identity.

What Does the Scientific Evidence Say?

It's almost impossible to have a constructive conversation about sex and gender without some awareness of the scientific discussion. So here are a few things that every thoughtful Christian should know.

First, scientific studies on the relationship between *sex* and *gender* (and gender dysphoria) are relatively new. It's not as if science has it all figured out and Christians just need to crawl out of their caves and see the light. Relying on our current knowledge to understand everything about transgender people or gender dysphoria is like asking a mechanic from 1915 to tell us everything we'll ever need to know about automobiles. It'll be years, if ever, before we fully understand the complexities of transgender experiences. Not only is the science still wet cement, but scientific theories and studies are much more diverse than some popular media makes them out to be.[1]

Second, there is no scientific evidence that your internal sense of self or your personal identity defines who you "really are" while your biology got it wrong. In fact, determining who you really are (a question about identity) is more of a theological endeavor than a scientific one. For Christians, the question isn't primarily: "Who do *I* think I am?" or "What does my internal sense of self tell me I am?" but "Who does my *Creator* say that I am, and how has he revealed that to me?" If you believe that the Bible is authoritative, and if you believe our bodies are intrinsic to who we are, then biological females *really are* female and biological males *really are* male—regardless of how we identify or experience life.

> There is no scientific evidence that your internal sense of self or your personal identity defines who you "really are" while your biology got it wrong.

But if you believe that a person's psychological experience trumps the Bible and biology, then you might say that a biological male could actually be a female. One writer puts it like this: "Our internal sense of ourselves is considered to be more indicative of who we are than our bodies."[2] If you agree with this, then there's no need for scientific evidence. All you need is to embrace your "internal sense" of who you think you are, even if your biology disagrees.

Some people, however, *do* want to show that transgender identities are rooted in biology. The most popular theory to date is the so-called "brain-sex theory," which suggests that some people born male might have a female brain, and vice versa. The theory has become quite popular, but it rests on shaky evidence and has been criticized by liberal and conservative scientists alike.[3] At the very least, many more independent studies need to be done in order to bolster the scientific credibility of "brain-sex theory."[4]

Simply put, there is no conclusive evidence that a genetic female really can be a man, or vice versa. Drs. Lawrence Mayer and Paul McHugh, two prominent psychiatrists associated with Johns Hopkins University, who recently combed through all the research, draw a bold conclusion about gender identity and biology:

> [T]he idea that gender identity is an innate, fixed property of human beings that is independent of biological sex—that a person might be "a man

trapped in a woman's body" or "a woman trapped in a man's body"—is not supported by scientific evidence.[5]

Mayer and McHugh are often written off as being conservative and therefore biased (as if conservatives are the only ones who are biased), which is why the perspective of nonconservative scientists like Drs. Rebecca Jordan-Young and J. Michael Bailey is important. Both are pro LGBT+, and *both* have criticized the brain-sex theory on scientific grounds.[6] As has Dr. Anne Lawrence, who's an interesting figure. Dr. Lawrence is an accomplished psychologist with an MD and a PhD and is a world-renowned specialist on questions related to sexual orientation and gender identity. And she too has been very critical of the brain-sex theory from a scientific perspective, arguing: "It is time to abandon the brain-sex theory of transsexualism and to adopt a more plausible and clinically relevant theory in its place."[7] This is an interesting conclusion, given the fact that Dr. Lawrence herself identifies as transgender and has transitioned from male to female. You'd think she would want to argue for brain-sex theory, but she doesn't. From her perspective, the scientific evidence won't let her.

To date, there is no credible scientific evidence that any given biological man is truly a woman (or vice versa). There *is* evidence—and piles of it—that people do experience life with intense, ongoing, debilitating, and in some cases life-threatening incongruence with their biological sex. Just a reminder: As we dissect the science, let us also imitate the scandalous compassion of Christ toward those who experience life against the grain of the way God intends it. Because, let's face it—we *all* do in one way or another.

> One of the most outspoken opponents of sex reassignment surgery is Walt Heyer, a man who formerly identified as a woman but now regrets ever getting a sex change.

Third, one's "internal sense of who they are" is often fluid and not fixed—that is, their experience doesn't appear to be innately coded into their humanity like the color of their eyes. (Their biological sex, however, is.) This is especially true in kids. According to the eleven studies that have followed children who experience gender dysphoria, 60–90 percent of those who struggle end up identifying with their biological sex by adulthood.[8] This is why some scientists say they are "disturbed and alarmed by the severity and irreversibility of some interventions being publicly discussed and employed for children."[9]

My friend Kyla, for instance, has struggled with gender incongruence most of her life. Six years ago, she began cross sex hormone therapy and sex reassignment surgery and began to identify as a man. But in the last few months, she's experienced a driving desire to identify with her birth sex once again. Now she's in the process of detransitioning—more hormones and surgeries to realign her body with her birth sex.

Kyla is part of a growing number of people experiencing "transition regret"—wishing they hadn't taken such invasive measure to align their bodies with their gender experience. One of the most outspoken opponents of sex reassignment surgery is Walt Heyer, a man who formerly identified as a woman but now regrets ever getting a sex change. Heyer has interviewed several doctors who have performed hundreds of sex reassignment surgeries and who say that such surgery is not as effective as some people think at relieving gender dysphoria or providing a higher quality of life. For instance, Charles Ihlenfeld is an endocrinologist who's administered cross-sex hormones to more than five hundred transgender patients but has recently stopped. He believes that 80 percent of people seeking hormone therapy shouldn't do it: "There is too much unhappiness among people who have had the surgery.... Too many end in suicide."[10]

The moral of the story is: Even from a purely scientific point of view, one's gender identity (i.e., one's internal

Even from a purely scientific point of view, one's gender identity (i.e. one's internal sense of self) shifts and changes—especially for people under twenty-five years old. It's not coded into our DNA as our biological sex is. Moreover—*there are people who experience intense gender dysphoria throughout their entire life* and whose cross-gender experience never changes. There's no pill they can take that makes it go away, no formula to follow, no counselor with a magic answer. I can't think of a greater need than for the church to *be* the church toward people struggling with gender dysphoria—to swallow them up with the love of Christ and to walk with them night and day in the grace and truth of our Savior.

What about Intersex Persons?

That brings us to the question of intersex. It never fails—whenever people say that male and female aren't the only two options, they quickly bring up people who are intersex.

A Grace/Truth Response to the Gender Conversation | 119

Intersex is "a general term used for a variety of conditions in which a person is born with a reproductive or sexual anatomy that doesn't seem to fit the typical definitions of female or male."[11] There are several different conditions classified as intersex, which affect approximately one out of every 4,500 people.[12]

So does this mean that one out of every 4,500 people aren't male or female? Here are three things to keep in mind.

First, intersex people are *people* and it's actually dehumanizing to use such people as a pawn to support an ideology. And even if genuinely intersex people are rare, from a Christian perspective their rarity should *increase,* not *decrease,* our passion to extend the love of Christ to them and reassure them that they are beautiful creations who bear God's image. Jesus left the ninety-nine to love the one, and so should we. Normalcy and popularity are given new meaning in the shadow of the cross.

Second, we have to be clear on what intersex is. Most intersex persons are not *unambiguously sexed*. This is so important to note, because some people flippantly refer to intersex persons as if they are neither male nor female. Except in very rare cases, people identified as intersex are still observably male or female—much of the ambiguity involved does not make sexual identification impossible. For instance, males—and they are classified as males—with Klinefelter's syndrome are hardly distinguishable from other unaffected males.[13] They are typically infertile and have smaller testicles, but they are still unambiguously male, even though they are classified as intersex. Vaginal agenesis is another intersex condition that is characterized by an underdeveloped vagina and the absence of menstruation, and yet those with this condition are, in every other way, unambiguously female.[14]

Intersex conditions where the sex of the person is more significantly blurred are extremely rare. Someone with complete androgen insensitivity syndrome (CAIS) has XY (male) chromosomes but female sexual anatomy, though their internal reproductive organs are often impaired or nonexistent. In appearance, they look unambiguously female. In fact, some with CAIS don't even know they have it until they are young adults. CAIS affects one in thirteen thousand people.[15]

In sum, every human born into this world bears God's image in unique and beautiful ways. We shouldn't highlight the rarity of some types of conditions in a way that could "other" certain people. We also shouldn't use rare conditions like these to construct completely different categories of biological sex. These conditions reveal medically explained disorders in sex development, not examples of another sex.

Third, the fact that some people are born with abnormalities in their biological sex should not be surprising. Some people are born with cleft lips, missing limbs, and all sorts of atypical biological features. In fact, I was born deaf in my left ear. All this means is that sin has affected the very fabric of our being, and sometimes it distorts our biology—even from birth. It doesn't mean that I belong in a different class of one-eared humans. Some people are born with their legs connected to each other for all or most of their length, a condition that affects one in twelve thousand people—about the same as the intersex condition of CAIS. But this doesn't mean that humans aren't bipedal. Biological abnormalities at birth are products of a fallen world—something we *all* experience in one way or another. It shouldn't surprise us that our sexual anatomy, reproductive organs, or even our chromosomes have been touched by the fall.

In all of this, we must have compassion and empathy for anyone whose biological abnormalities might be causing some level of psychological distress. (By the way, it's rather insulting to assume that all intersex people are suffering distress or struggling with their sexual identity.) I don't think we should hold up intersex persons as evidence that male and female aren't the only two options, or to prove that transgender people really are a gender different from their biological sex.

Navigating the Bathroom Debate

Before we discuss some relational "so whats?" we can't forget about that elephant in the room—male and female bathrooms.

Sex-specific facilities are one of the more contentious issues in this discussion. Traditionally, public bathrooms and changing places have been segregated based on biological sex for the sake of bodily privacy. Recent bathroom laws in various states, however, allow biological men to use female bathrooms if they identify as females (or vice versa for biological women). I offer the following thoughts to help initiate a discussion at the end of this conversation, not to solve this unsolvable discussion.

Personally, I don't think it's helpful to base bathroom usage on gender identity rather than biological sex. But because that is becoming common in the world we live in, Christians need to think through these issues on at least two different levels. First, the public level. Second, the private religious level.

By "public level," I'm talking about how Christians should think about various businesses and public places that now segregate bathrooms by gender identity rather than biological sex. Some Christians are eager to boycott businesses like Target and others that allow people to use the bathroom of their choice. I'm a big fan of following your convictions, but if you desire to boycott a store for this, just make sure you're being consistent and boycotting all stores that have what you would see as immoral or harmful policies. For instance, China has some very inhumane child labor practices, and yet many American businesses sell products made by Chinese child slaves. Should you boycott those stores too? I take the approach that Christians are servants of God living in Babylon, and this nation—wherever you live—is not our home. We should never expect Babylon to look like the New Jerusalem.

As far as safety goes, there are several examples of men, claiming a transgender identity, who take advantage of the recent bathroom policies and violate women in female bathrooms.[16] But there has always been some level of risk when using a public bathroom—long before the recent changes in bathroom policies. Girls have been raped by men in female bathrooms, and boys have been raped by men in male bathrooms. This has always been a horrific possibility. As one retired sheriff says: "Public restrooms are crime attractors, and have long been well-known as areas in which offenders seek out victims in a planned and deliberate way."[17] I don't agree with segregating bathrooms based on gender rather than on biological sex. But as a parent with four kids, I've *always* been cautious about public bathrooms, long before recent change of laws.

So, what about private religious environments? How should churches approach their own bathroom policies?

I think that bathrooms and sleeping arrangements (on youth trips, for instance) should be based on biological sex, not gender identity or sexual attraction. After all, sex-specific facilities have always been established for the purpose of bodily privacy. Plus, with so many gender options and sexual identities, how many bathrooms are we willing to build? Unless I see a better argument otherwise, it seems best to segregate people according to their biological sex and not the infinite number of other identities.

There will always be messy situations that defy easy responses, such as: What do we do about the individual who has transitioned and now has the physical appearance of the sex opposite their birth? But as a general rule, when there is male/female separation in a religious environment, I think there are far better theological and social reasons to base the division on biological sex, for the sake of bodily privacy, and not on gender identity.

I offer those thoughts as a discussion starter for your group to interact with when you discuss the questions at the end of this conversation.

Loving Your Transgender Neighbor—the Grace/Truth Way

Let's move from science and policies to navigating the grace/truth way of Jesus. Or—how can you love your transgender neighbor? Here are four relational principles to keep tucked away in your heart.

1. Humanize the discussion

It's easy for emotions to get heated when discussing political bathroom policies and Tumblr's 117 gender options. But next time you get frazzled over what seems to be the latest gender trend or ideological fad, just remember—there's a twelve-year-old kid in your church who is seriously thinking of putting a gun to his head because he feels more feminine than masculine, and he has no one to talk to. When you lay your head on your warm pillow at night, remember that there are dozens, if not hundreds, of homeless LGBT+ youth wandering the streets of your city at night. When you're singing praises to Jesus next Sunday, there's a good chance that there are two or three or twenty people in the same sanctuary who struggle with their gender identity on some level, and no one knows about it. They might be the worship leader, the greeter, the person who served you coffee, or the pastor's wife.

We cannot just be vigilant about resisting unbiblical cultural ideologies. Yes, we should resist. But we must also care for people who are struggling and in need of love. And we can't let our frustration over political debates and biased news articles snuff out our unswerving passion for people.

2. Understand the diversity

One of our running themes throughout *Grace/Truth 1.0* and *2.0* is diversity. There are many different types of LGBT+ people. We need to shred our stereotypes and get to know actual people. And the same goes for transgender (and other gender-nonconforming) people.

Gender researchers have distinguished at least four different types of transgender people, and it's important to consider the differences. First, there are people who have true *gender dysphoria*. For some, it's manageable, while for others it's utterly debilitating and life threatening. These are people who have a serious condition and often need professional help. If you get to know someone who falls in this category, you need to enter into this relationship with the utmost sensitivity and care. And I would recommend seeking professional guidance as you continue to walk with them.

Second, there are people who simply don't fit the cultural stereotypes of masculinity and femininity. Men who love musicals and art; women who hate to cook and love football. These cultural boxes are in many ways artificial, and yet they are still very real. Stereotypes don't determine your gender, but they do affect your self-perception. If someone whose behavior and tastes differ from cultural expectations for their gender walked into a psychiatrist's office, they might not leave with a prescription. But if they walked into your church, they'd better leave with a friend—one who can help them see through the cultural stereotypes and gaze upon the One who created them to be male or female.

Third, there are some people (usually biological men) whose transgender identity is a by-product of an erotic desire to envision themselves as a woman. (The scientific term for this is *autogynephilia*.) They are sexually turned on by envisioning themselves as a woman, and they may be sexually attracted to either men or women. They're often not stereotypically feminine, are usually married to a woman, have a history of cross dressing in secret, and often desire to transition later in life. The way you relate with this type of transgender person might be different than the other types of transgender persons. And by all means, please *don't* assume that all transgender people are in this category.

Lastly, there's a growing number of younger people who identify as transgender because, well, it's sort of trendy. And they typically have a huge heart for the marginalized and oppressed. And since transgender people have been marginalized and oppressed, some people identify as transgender in order to identify with the people they are standing up for. Dr. Stephen Stathis, an Australian psychiatrist who runs a gender clinic, said that only a minority of the transgender patients who come to him are actually diagnosed with gender dysphoria. Most don't truly, deep down, believe that they are a member of the opposite sex. One even said: "Dr. Steve … I want to be transgender, it's the new black."[18]

It's crucial to understand the different types of people who might identify as transgender or gender nonconforming. For instance, if your son or daughter comes out as transgender, they might be thinking, "It's the new black." You could misdiagnose the problem if you assume that they are experiencing severe gender dysphoria. Or the opposite could be more devastating: If you simply treat them as chasing some trend when in reality they are experiencing a debilitating psychological condition—that misdiagnosis could be life threatening for them. The key, of course, is to truly listen to their story. Maybe there's been a lot going on in their life that you didn't know about. Ask a thousand questions and be an eager listener—a student of their story. Get to know them from the inside out and wear their story like a tight-fitting garment. Yes, this might take hours or days or even years. But you won't know how to help them if you haven't taken the time to *truly know* them.

The point is—we must listen, love, listen, and keep on loving. Ask a thousand genuine questions. Reassure them that you will walk with them in this journey. Once you have a sense of what's going on deep down in their heart, you can then walk with them toward the best kind of help they need. If they are struggling with some intense sexual fetish or severe gender dysphoria (or both), then I would highly recommend seeking professional help.

3. Promote a biblical view of gender

I truly believe that our narrow, cultural definitions of masculinity and femininity contribute to the confusion around gender identity today. We need to speak against it. We must challenge the cultural status quo. We need to promote the beautiful freedom that God gives us through his word to express our maleness and femaleness in different ways. Again, sex difference matters. Men and women *are* beautifully different, and we cannot erase the differences! But neither should we create artificial differences or blindly follow cultural definitions of difference.

So what should we do? First, identify any nonbiblical, cultural notions of masculinity and femininity in your own thinking. Just because they may be cultural doesn't mean they're wrong. (I personally love sports, hunting, and red meat, though I don't think I'm more of a man because of these interests.) They can become wrong, though, if we force them upon others. There are questions at the end of this conversation that will help with this.

Second, if you have kids or people under your influence or leadership who may exhibit gender-nonconforming behaviors or interests, reassure them of their identity as male or female. Fathers especially have a hard time with this if they have a son who's not into cultural interests that define a man—hunting, fishing, sports, working on cars, etc. Fathers: If your son is into art or wants to sing in the choir instead of joining the football team, your attitude toward his interest will play a *significant* role in his self-perception. Mothers: If your daughter desires a career more than she wants to have kids, that's okay. God has a special place in his kingdom for women who don't fit the typical mold of motherhood (Judges 4).

If you look down upon your son or daughter, or make them feel like they're not living up to their (cultural standard of) gender, they'll probably look down upon themselves and feel less manly or womanly than they ought.

4. Befriend a person who identifies as transgender

My last piece of advice is a challenge. And I want you to take this seriously. If you don't already know someone who identifies as transgender, as nonbinary, or who experiences gender dysphoria, pray that God would bring such a person into your life. A friend, a relative, a coworker, a neighbor, or a fellow student. Since the gender conversation is so popular and important today, it's essential that Christians engage in it. We need to be informed and thoughtful. We've taken a tour through many issues over the last two conversations. Now it's time to move from seeing it on paper to getting to know it—or them—as people.

Pray earnestly that God would bring someone who fits that description into your life. Of course, God may choose not to do so. But if he does, then here are some ways in which you can be a friend.

First, listen like crazy. Hear their story. Ask good questions. Don't interrogate them. But ask honest questions that show you're eager to walk this journey with them.

Second, if you're unsure about what identity label to use or what terms you should or shouldn't say around them, simply ask them. It's rare that people get offended when someone humbly asks another person what pronouns or names or labels they should or shouldn't use.

> For a Christian perspective on using cross-gender pronouns, see the pastoral paper: "A Christian Perspective on the Pronoun Debate," available at centerforfaith.com/resources.

Third, speaking of pronouns ("he, she, they," etc.), I would recommend using whatever pronoun the person prefers, especially at the beginning of the relationship. I know this is uncomfortable for some, and many fear that doing so is a flagrant denial of truth. But here's the thing: if you try to begin a relationship by refusing to use their preferred pronouns, that will probably be the end of the relationship. And when your relationship with them ends, your ability to influence them ends as well. Think about this biblically. When God wanted to begin a relationship with us, he met us where we were at so that he could journey with us to where he wants us to be. We should follow the same pattern. We should meet people where they are so that God can use us to journey with them into the person God intends they become.

QUESTIONS FOR DISCUSSION

1. What impression have you gotten about transgender people from media? Do you personally know any transgender people who are openly advocating for special treatment?

2. If someone who identifies as transgender came to your church and asked the leadership for permission to use the bathroom not of their biological sex but of their gender identity, how do you think your leadership should respond?

3. If a biological male who identified as female wanted to go on a mission trip, how would you recommend leaders handle sleeping, bathroom, and shower arrangements?

4. Discuss the morality of straight people having breast implants, in vitro fertilization, or vasectomies versus sex reassignment surgery and cross-sex hormone therapy for people who identify as transgender. Is there a difference? Why or why not?

5. What questions do you have about intersex people? Do you agree that such a condition is the result of being born into a fallen world? Or do you see intersex persons as a third or other sex that's different from male or female?

6. We talked about the need for awareness that there are different types of transgender people. What are some godly, sensitive, respectful approaches you might take to increase your awareness of which type your new transgender friend is?

7. In this chapter, I suggested that you "first, identify any nonbiblical, cultural notions of masculinity and femininity in your own thinking." Can you think of any? Start by listing any ideas about masculine or feminine cultural traits or roles, any at all. Then go through your list and identify those that don't seem to have any bibical basis and that seem to be linked to cultural norms instead.

8. What can you do in your church to raise awareness about cultural stereotypes of masculinity and femininity? How can you promote biblical views of masculinity and femininity?

9. If someone came to your church whose gender looked ambiguous, how would you approach them? What questions would you ask? How would you make them feel welcomed?

10. Near the end of this conversation, I recommend that, when speaking to someone who identifies as transgender, you use whichever pronouns—he, she, his, her—correspond to the gender with which that person identifies, regardless of biological sex. Whether you've already attempted this or not, discuss the problems this may create for you. Would this create no particular problem? Would you feel that you were being untrue before the God who created this person? Would you feel that you were contributing to his or her gender confusion?

ENDNOTES

1 For a rather frightening read of how ideology can interrupt (or sometimes persecute) genuine scientific inquiry, read Alice Dreger's *Galileo's Middle Finger: Heretics, Activists, and the Search for Justice in Science* (New York: Penguin Press, 2015).

2 Linda Tatro Herzer, *The Bible and the Transgender Experience: How Scripture Supports Gender Variance* (Cleveland: The Pilgrim Press, 2016), 62.

3 There are at least two methodological problems with this theory. First, the most influential studies rely on a very small sample size—six male-to-female and seven female-to-male people. For a scientific theory to be valid, it would need a much larger sample size. Second, in most studies, the subjects were examined postmortem and they had taken hormones throughout their life. It's unclear, therefore, whether their brains really were opposite-sex brains or whether taking hormones made them this way (since taking hormones will affect your brain).

4 After Mark Yarhouse surveyed all the relevant studies done on causation, he concluded: "It seems wise to consider any model of causation with some humility, almost holding it in an open hand with an understanding that we may know more in the years to come that will help us understand this topic better than we do today" (*Understanding Gender Dysphoria: Navigating Transgender Issues in a Changing Culture* (Downers Grove: IVP Academic, 2015), 79.

5 Lawrence Mayer and Paul McHugh, "Sexuality and Gender: Findings from the Biological, Psychological, and Social Sciences," *The New Atlantis* (2016), 8.

6 J. Michael Bailey and Kiira Triea, "What Many Transgender Activists Don't Want You to Know: and why you should know it anyway," *Perspectives in Biology and Medicine* 50 (2007): 521–34.

7 http://rodfleming.com/wp-content/uploads/2016/07/A-Critique-of-the-Brain-Sex-Theory-of-Transsexualism-2007.pdf.

8 http://www.sexologytoday.org/2016/01/do-trans-kids-stay-trans-when-they-grow_99.html. See also: *American College of Pediatricians* (Aug 2016), www.ACPeds.org and the discussion by Dr. Deborah Soh: https://www.theglobeandmail.com/opinion/dont-treat-all-cases-of-gender-dysphoria-the-same-way/article 37711831.

Drs. Mayer and McHugh agree: "Only a minority of children who experience cross-gender identification will continue to do so into adolescence or adulthood" (Mayer and McHugh, "Sexuality and Gender," 9).

9 Mayer and McHugh, "Sexuality and Gender," 12.

10 http://www.thepublicdiscourse.com/2015/04/14905.

11 http://www.isna.org/faq/what_is_intersex.

12 There's a massive debate among intersex specialists about how many people are genuinely born intersex. A consensus statement constructed by a team of almost fifty specialists, who have analyzed all the data, concluded that about 0.22 percent of all live births are intersex; that is, one in every 4,500. See I. A. Hughes, C. Houk, S. F. Ahmed, P. A. Lee, and LWPES/ESPE [Lawson Wilkins Pediatric Endocrine Society/European Society for Paediatric Endocrinology] Consensus Group, "Consensus Statement on Management of Intersex Disorders," *Archives of Disease in Childhood* 2 (2006): 1–11. www.archdischild.com.

13 https://www.nichd.nih.gov/health/topics/klinefelter/conditioninfo/Pages/symptoms.aspx.

14 http://www.childrenshospital.org/conditions-and-treatments/conditions/vaginal-agenesis.

15 The condition called ovotestes (where the person, as you might guess, has both ovarian and testicular tissue) affects 1 in 83,000.

16 Ryan T. Anderson has documented 130 cases where men have sexually assaulted women or children in female facilities. In some of the more recent cases, the perpetrators said they identified as transgender or used the new laws to gain access to the facilities: https://www.heritage.org/education/report/gender-identity-policies-schools-what-congress-the-courts-and-the-trump.

17 Cited by Ryan T. Anderson, *When Harry Became Sally: Responding to the Transgender Moment* (New York: Encounter, 2018), 186.

18 https://honey.nine.com.au/2017/04/10/14/39/psychiatrist-notes-increase-in-childrens-use-of-transgender-as-way-to-be-different.

CONVERSATION 10

LGBT+ Inclusion in the Church

Congratulations! You've made it through nine conversations about faith, sexuality & gender! If all has gone as planned, you'll have learned some things you didn't know and had some beliefs reaffirmed, while others might have been challenged. Hopefully you've also had some questions answered, and I'm sure that what we've discussed has raised other questions you didn't know you had. Most of all, I hope and pray that *Grace/Truth 1.0* and *2.0* have cultivated more passion to love and care for LGBT+ people and their families in a way that honors both the grace and truth of God as revealed through Scripture.

I want to begin this final conversation with a scenario. Let's say a lesbian couple named Gina and Kayla start coming to your church. They love the preaching and the worship and build relationships with several people at your church. After a few months of attending, they make a confession to accept Jesus as Lord and Savior, and now they want to become members and use their talents to serve within the church. Gina is musically gifted and wants to serve on the worship team. Kayla has a huge heart for the poor and would love to serve at your church's Saturday morning outreach to the homeless.

How would you feel about them becoming members and serving on the worship team and homeless ministry at your church?

We'll return to this question at the end of this conversation. But in order to think through it more clearly, there are other things we need to wrestle with—specifically, these three questions:

1. Is the debate about same-sex relations a primary or a secondary issue?

2. How should Christians who hold to a traditional view of marriage relate to affirming Christians?

3. Can affirming LGBT+ Christians become members and serve at your church?

The first two questions are relevant for everyday relationships among Christians, and they also relate directly to the membership question. Once we wrestle with these two, then we can think through the third question about membership.

I want you to know up front than there's no clear black-and-white answer to these questions, so don't expect to walk away from this last conversation with some quick-and-easy answer to these complex questions. My goal is not to give you "*the* right answer" but to give you the proper framework to wrestle with these questions in your own relational context. I also want you to appreciate how godly, faithful Christian leaders can respond differently to these questions—and still be godly and faithful.

Is the Debate about Same-Sex Relations a Primary or a Secondary Issue?

Every Christian believes some doctrines are more important, or clearer in Scripture, than others. For instance, some Christians believe in what's called a pretribulation rapture, where believers will be caught up to heaven right before a seven-year end-time period of tribulation. Christians who believe this, though, will usually say that this doctrine isn't as crucial to the Christian faith as is the deity of Christ or salvation by grace.

Whether it's a pretrib rapture, adult versus infant baptism, or the question of whether Christians should ever drink alcohol, some things aren't as important as others.

Instead of placing every doctrine in one of two categories—primary or secondary—it's better to place them somewhere along a continuum with primary and secondary at opposite ends, so that it looks like this:

Primary   **Secondary**

Deity of Christ   Adult vs. infant baptism   Timing of the rapture

In this example, I put "adult vs. infant baptism" somewhere in the middle. Most Christians would say that one's beliefs about baptism (adult vs. infant) isn't essential for salvation, and yet whole denominations like the Southern Baptist Convention or the Presbyterian Church of America have been formed around where they stand on this issue. Looking at Christendom as a whole, baptism can't be neatly placed into either a primary or secondary category, which is why it's best to view it somewhere in the middle of the spectrum.

This brings us to our question: Is the historically Christian view of marriage (one man and one woman) more of a *primary* doctrine like the deity of Christ, or closer to a *secondary* doctrine like the timing of the rapture? As you reflect on this question, it's important to give good reasons for your view.

I encourage you to form your own opinions on this and to feel free to agree or disagree with mine, but here's how I would answer this question.

I don't believe that the debate about same-sex marriage is a secondary issue. I'm not ready to say it's on par with the deity of Christ, and I wouldn't say you can't be a Christian and be affirming. But I do think it's closer to being a primary issue than a secondary one. Here's why.

First, marriage in Scripture is described as a one-flesh union between sexually different persons (Gen. 2:18–24; Matt. 19:3–5). It's one of the few things God instituted before the Fall, and it's consistently taught throughout Scripture with no variation.[1] Also, the institution of marriage is absolutely crucial to the health (and existence!) of human civilization. From ancient times to the present, this pattern has held: When marriage begins to break down, so does society.[2]

Second, whenever same-sex sexual relations are mentioned, they are condemned and considered to be sexually immoral (Lev. 18:22; 20:13; Rom. 1:26–27; 1 Cor. 6:9; 1 Tim. 1:10). There is no variation in this, and no other verses suggest the opposite—that same-sex sexual relations might be sanctified under some context.

Consider those first two points in light of other things that most Christians would consider to be secondary issues: the rapture, drinking, modes of baptism, election, whether divorce is ever permitted, and others. One of the things that makes these issues secondary is that you can find Scripture passages that support each view held by groups of Christians. But this simply isn't true with same-sex relationships. There's no diversity or variation in Scripture. There's no verse that says something positive about same-sex relations and no passage that says marriage is between two consenting adults regardless of sex difference.

Scripture is remarkably uniform and consistent in what it says about same-sex sexual relationships.

Third, there has been a global, multidenominational, two-thousand-year agreement on this question.

LGBT+ Inclusion in the Church | 149

Catholics, Protestants, Greek Orthodox, Russian Orthodox, Coptic Christians—cast the net as broadly as you want, and you will find no variation for two thousand years. African Christians, Asian Christians, rich Christians, poor Christians. Christians in majority-world (formerly called "third-world") countries, and Christians living in first-world countries. Wherever Christianity has existed, Christians have always believed that marriage is between sexually different people and that same-sex relations were sin. Until very recently, the official stance of every group and denomination of Christians, from Catholics to snake-handling charismatics to KJV-only fundamentalists, has been that sex difference is a necessary part of marriage.

> Until very recently, the official stance of every group and denomination of Christians, from Catholics to snake-handling charismatics to KJV-only fundamentalists, has been that sex difference is a necessary part of marriage.

It's only been in the last few decades in the West (among mostly white people) that some Christians have suggested that everyone else globally and historically has had it wrong all these years. This global, historical, two-thousand-year-long consensus suggests that it isn't some secondary issue. Secondary issues find all kinds of different opinions throughout historic, global Christianity. We don't see this with same-sex relations.

Lastly, Scripture never considers issues of sexual immorality to be a secondary issue that good Christians can shake hands and agree to disagree on (see 1 Cor. 6:9, 18; Eph. 5:5). Christ himself comes down particularly hard on those who not only engage in sexual immorality but teach others that some form of sexual immorality is okay (Rev. 2:14, 20). It's true that some ethical practices might be considered secondary. In fact, the very first church council in Acts 15 was devoted to figuring out what's essential and what's not essential for Gentiles who want to become Christians. And one of the few things that Gentiles were required to do was to "abstain ... from sexual immorality" (*porneia*, Acts 15:20, 29)—a word that included same-sex sexual relations.

So, with leaders of the early church, I don't think same-sex sexual relations were a secondary issue. But please: Test my reasoning. Think through my evidence. It's important that you think through this question for yourself, because how you answer it will affect the way you relate to people who disagree with you.

This leads to our second question.

How Should Christians Who Hold to a Traditional View of Marriage Relate to Affirming Christians?

I want to be upfront and honest with you. I've been thinking through this question for several years, and the more I think about it, the tougher it gets! Part of my goal is to help you see how complicated it is so that you can cultivate humility and grace as you talk about these issues with other Christians. It's helpful to recognize that there are different types of affirming Christians. They're not all the same, and they might require different relational approaches.

1. Straight and privately affirming

This is a Christian who is straight and affirming but not vocal about it. They may not agree with you or your church's view of same-sex relations, but you would never know it unless you ask. They're not looking to argue or to promote their views. And since they're straight, they personally are not engaging in same-sex sexual relationships.

2. Straight and publicly affirming

This person is much like the one we just discussed except they are vocal about their views. They're probably well studied on the issues, and they publicize their views on social media and in casual conversations. They're passionate about the topic and probably consider the historically Christian view of marriage dehumanizing and bigoted. But like the first person, they are straight and therefore aren't engaging in same-sex sexual immorality.

3. LGBT+, affirming, and not yet in a sexual relationship

This person is gay, lesbian, bisexual, or transgender and is not currently in a relationship. However, they are open to pursuing a same-sex relationship in the future. They still believe that sex outside of marriage is sin, and so they are not sleeping around. But they believe that same-sex marriages are not sin and are very much open to pursuing such a relationship in the future.

4. LGBT+, affirming, and in a sexual relationship

This person *is* currently in a same-sex sexual relationship. This relationship may be a legal marriage, or it may be nonmarital. Either way, this person is a confessing Christian and is currently in a sexual relationship that you consider to be immoral.

I wish I could give you a definite, unassailable answer to our question above, a 2 +2 = 4 answer, but relationships don't work that way. Relationships are more like art than arithmetic, so we should not expect a black-and-white answer to our question. With that in mind, here are four things to consider as you navigate relationships with your affirming friends.

First, almost all (like 99.5 percent, I would guess) affirming Christians have a huge heart for LGBT+ people. Affirming Christians are typically distraught over how LGBT+ people have been dehumanized and mistreated by the church, and they desire to create a church culture where the marginalized are welcome and cherished. As you relate to your affirming friends, please realize—*these are wonderful desires and you should affirm them as such.* Even though I believe that affirming same-sex marriage runs contrary to God's intention, I also believe that there are good motivations fueling a person to affirm same-sex marriage.

Relationally, you should celebrate whatever good motivations you see in them. This does *not* mean you agree with their views or that you should downplay the severity of the disagreement. It just means you're willing to see past their views and into their heart. After all, don't you want them to take the same attitude toward you? To understand and respect the fact that you are giving your allegiance to God and his Word; that you're not a bigot and don't hate gay people; that you're trying to think and act faithfully to God's design for marriage?

Affirm the good in people while being honest with the disagreement.

Second, I think that the first three types of affirming Christians are somewhat different from the fourth. None of the first three are engaging in sexual immorality, so they're not violating scriptural prohibitions against same-sex sexual behavior. While the Bible has much to say about Christians living in unrepentant, ongoing sin (see below), it's not as clear about how to relate to Christians who *believe against* but aren't *behaving against* a Christian sexual ethic.

There are some passages that come down hard against applauding the sinful behavior of others (Rom. 1:32; Rev. 2:14). But these passages focus on people who *know very well* what is right and what is wrong, who are themselves participating in such sinful behavior, and who are encouraging the same sinful behavior in others. Not every affirming Christian would fit this description.

Also, we're living in a distinct cultural moment where there's much confusion about Christian sexual ethics, and the church hasn't always done the best job at articulating God's design for sex and marriage. At least some affirming Christians are simply following what their leaders are telling them. In some ways, they might be both victims and culprits—victims of living under poor teachers who have fed them bad theology, and culprits for believing such theology. But it's not as if they are willfully rejecting God's truth. They simply haven't been correctly taught what that truth is. I'm more eager to build and maintain a relationship with affirming Christians who have this sort of background.

I have a harder time continuing a relationship with any confessing Christian—gay or straight—who holds onto their affirming view with pomp and pride. And, by the way, I've also come across quite a few traditional Christians who hold their view with pomp and pride and a whole lot of ignorance—they adamantly declare *what* they believe, but don't really know why. Pride is pride, arrogance is arrogance, regardless of your view of marriage.

Some affirming Christians hold their view humbly, and as far as I can tell, they've arrived at their view through rigorous study, much prayer, and in dialogue with other Christians. But I have a hard time relating to people who boldly trumpet the affirming view while scoffing at the global church for believing otherwise. It's not even really about their affirming view. It's the stubborn heart that's fueling it. I still want to see what kind of pain or trauma might be shaping their posture. We're told that "a gentle answer turns away wrath" (Prov. 15:1 NIV). But we're also encouraged to "not speak to fools, for they will scorn your prudent words" (Prov. 23:9 NIV). Deciding which approach to take in any given moment takes a good dose of wisdom salted with the Spirit's leading.

Third, the New Testament does talk about that topic no one wants to mention—church discipline. In 1 Corinthians 5, Paul rebukes the church for tolerating one of its members for living in unrepentant sexual immorality and commands them to "purge the evil person from among you" (1 Cor. 5:13). This sounds harsh, and maybe it is, but it also shows how important it was for Paul (and other Christian leaders) that the church pursue purity and holiness. Not perfection, mind you! We'll all enter heaven with a limp, and no one should be expected to live a perfect life. But there's a big difference between struggling with sin and calling sin righteousness.

Now, here's where it gets tricky. While in 1 Corinthians 5 Paul singles out sexual sin, he goes on to tell them to "not associate with anyone who claims to be a brother or sister but is sexually immoral or greedy, an idolater or slanderer, a drunkard or swindler. Do not even eat with such people" (1 Cor. 5:11 NIV). However you interpret this passage, you must equally apply it to greedy people, idolaters, slanderers—including on Facebook and Instagram—drunkards and swindlers.

In applying this passage, we have to keep in mind that Paul's instruction is directed at members of a particular local church, a church that probably consisted of thirty or forty people who were doing life together on a regular basis. As we apply Paul's words, we should stay as close to this original context as we can. Paul's not envisioning someone sitting in the ninety-fifth row of a megachurch on Sunday with no other real connection to their spiritual family. He's thinking of someone who's been part of a tight-knit spiritual family, who knows the standards of that family, yet who decides to live against those standards with no desire to change. In situations similar to these, yes, I believe that the most faithful biblical response is, as Paul says, to "not associate with" the person who persists in violating biblical sexual standards while claiming to be a Christian. But remember: be consistent. Don't single out those in same-sex relationships. Don't associate with "anyone who claims to be a brother or sister but is sexually immoral or greedy, an idolater or slanderer, a drunkard or swindler" (1 Cor. 5:11 NIV).

Fourth, does this mean that affirming, noncelibate gay Christians aren't saved? I definitely wouldn't go that far. Christians can have serious blind spots or sins in their life, and this doesn't in itself negate their salvation. Plus, I'm not a huge fan of making judgment calls on everyone's salvation, especially people I've never met. And yet the Bible raises serious questions about the salvation of those who claim to be believers and yet persist in what is clearly sin.

Therefore, I think it's best to avoid two extremes—judging everyone's salvation on the one hand, and pretending like behavior doesn't matter on the other. We are called to love people well; call out sin where it exists, *beginning with our own sin*; and let God determine who will be judged and who will enter eternal life.

With that in mind, let's talk about church membership.

Can Affirming Christians Become Members and Serve at Your Church?

Our third question is most pertinent for church leaders, since they're the ones ultimately making decisions about church membership requirements and about who is allowed to serve within the church. Now, even though *Grace/Truth 2.0* isn't written just to leaders, I assume that at least some readers are in leadership roles at their church or other Christian organization. Plus, when leaders make decisions, nonleaders are affected. So even if you're not in a position to make these sorts of decisions, it'll be good for you to consider this question.

Just to be clear, we're talking about *affirming* Christians— some of whom will be gay, lesbian, bisexual, transgender, or queer. When it comes to LGBT+ Christians *who believe in and live by* a historically Christian view of marriage and sexuality, *all* levels of membership, service, and leadership should be open to such people. If you're squeamish about a gay Christian who's living a sexually pure life and believes in a traditional view of marriage becoming a member or leader or pastor at your church, then I would highly recommend rereading *Grace/Truth 1.0*. There's nothing in the Bible which says that a sexually pure Christian is barred from certain positons of service, even if they are same-sex attracted.

Now, as we wrestle with affirming LGBT+ Christians and membership, we should keep in mind the four different types of affirming Christians: (1) straight and personally affirming, (2) straight and publicly affirming, (3) LGBT+, affirming, and not yet in a sexual relationship, and (4) LGBT+, affirming, and in a sexual relationship. Whether any one of these can become members depends on two different things. First, whether your church views same-sex marriage as more of a primary or more of a secondary issue. And second, how your church understands membership.

We've already talked about the spectrum of primary and secondary issues. If your church believes that same-sex marriage is more of a secondary issue, then they will inevitably be more lenient on requiring members or even leaders to believe in male/female marriage. This is where it can get complicated. You may think you know where your church stands on questions of marriage and sexuality, but do you know where they would place these questions on the spectrum of primary-secondary beliefs? If they see those questions as a secondary issue, then they might be okay with an affirming Christian becoming an elder, even though the church doesn't believe that same-sex marriage is okay.

If you are serving in leadership at your church and you have an opportunity to dialog with your congregation about membership or service for LGBT+ Christians, it would be helpful to talk about the primary-secondary spectrum and where your church lines up. This could clear up some confusion, especially if you decide to hire—or fire—a youth pastor who holds to a different view on marriage.

Churches also need to think through the expectations and requirements of membership. The categories that I've found to be helpful are what I call "high-buffer" membership and "low-buffer" membership.

"High-buffer" churches are harder to join, but once people are inside the circle, they often share a stronger group identity. Think, for example, of the military: There is a high bar of commitment for entrance, an expectation of significant sacrifice, and a standard of laying down your life for others within the circle. While it's harder to join, military troops are famous for the unbreakable, lifelong bond they share once inside. High-buffer churches expect their members to line up with the church's doctrine and ethical standard in order to join and serve.

"Low-buffer" churches are easier to get into but may have a weaker common identity. Think, for example, of a nightclub: there's easy access, anyone can join (assuming you're over twenty-one), and it's more inviting for a broader array of people. Low-buffer churches typically don't require people to line up with the church's doctrine or ethical standard in order to join and serve.

Again, I think it's helpful to think of high buffer and low buffer as points on a spectrum rather than two distinct categories.

Low buffer **High buffer**

Low expectations for belief and behavior — High expectations for belief and behavior

I won't say that one type of membership is better than another. I only want to encourage churches to reflect on their membership policy and—this is important—*consistently apply it to all people*. So, if you won't allow a lesbian couple to serve on your worship team, then you'd better not let your drummer, who's sleeping with his girlfriend, serve either. Membership policies shouldn't be about excluding gay people because they're gay. It should be about holding everyone to the same standard of belief and behavior.

After wrestling with all of these questions, and the questions within the questions, I hope you can appreciate the fact there's no quick and easy answer to them. It's no wonder that most pastors and leaders get gray hair early! If you're a pastor or leader, I hope that this conversation so far will help you clarify your membership and service policy. If you're not a pastor or leader, I think it's still very important to wrestle with these questions about membership and service, because they affect everyone in the church.

> For a more thorough discussion of the ideas discussed in this conversation, see the pastoral paper: "Guidance for Churches on Membership, Baptism, Communion, Leadership, and Service for Gay and Lesbian People," available for free at centerforfaith.com/resources.

With that in mind, let's revisit the scenario about Gina and Kayla—the lesbian couple who want to become members and serve at the church—I mentioned at the beginning of the chapter.

Can Gina and Kayla Join and Serve?

I'll tell you some of my own thoughts about their situation. But first, I want you to wrestle with it on your own. (Please do so *before* reading my thoughts below.) As you do, reflect on some of the questions that we considered above: (1) Are same-sex relations more of a primary or secondary issue, and why? (2) Is your church's membership and service policy (if it has one) more low buffer or high buffer? Once you've formulated a response to those questions with regard to your church, respond to the question about Gina and Kayla becoming members and serving.

_____

_____

_____

_____

_____

_____

_____

_____

_____

_____

// // //

Here are some of my own thoughts about Gina and Kayla's situation.

First, the number one thing I want to reiterate yet again is that Gina and Kayla (since we're assuming here that they are real people who have shown up at your church) are not some situation or issue or threat to a membership policy. They're beautiful people, made in God's image, who have value and worth and a desperate need to know Jesus and be loved by his people. The first thing I'd want to do, then, is make sure I get to know Gina and Kayla. What's their story? What's their background? What are their hopes and dreams and likes and dislikes? I'd want to go out of my way to befriend them, have them over for a few meals, invite them into my life, and show them that however we respond to their questions about membership and service, it's in the context of a real relationship. Even if you say no to membership, this doesn't have to mean no to a relationship.

Second, whenever an LGBT+ person expresses a desire to belong to a church, this is a massive step! There's a good chance they've experienced past rejection from other churches or other Christians. If so, and if you think they can't join or serve at your church, then you need to communicate this in such a way that it doesn't destroy their faith and make them feel like they're not wanted at your church.

Third, low-buffer churches will probably have no problem letting Gina and Kayla join and serve. Even though those churches may believe that same-sex relations are sin, they don't require members or those who serve to line up on everything the church believes. My one major caution for low-buffer churches is this: avoid the bait and switch. That is, don't hide your beliefs about same-sex relations from this couple, even if they're still allowed to serve. You don't want them to find out later what you really believe because you were too afraid to tell them earlier. Better to have a tough conversation up front than an even tougher one down the road.

If a high-buffer church considers same-sex relations to be more of a secondary issue, then it too might be eager to have Gina and Kayla join and serve.

So far, so good. None of the possibilities in the previous two paragraphs have shown much likelihood of conflict. But the last possibility—a high-buffer church that considers same-sex relations to be more of a primary issue—may struggle more than the others about what to do with Gina and Kayla.

Here are a few possible options for such high-buffer churches.

- The two women can both join and serve, but they would have to end their sexual relationship and their marriage. This sounds incredibly harsh, and Gina and Kayla might be appalled at this suggestion. But if a church requires all other members to agree with and try to live up to the church's standard of sexual morality, then, if they're consistent, they should apply this to all members and not just some. Some might wonder: Isn't it sin to say that Gina and Kayla must divorce in order to join the church? Not necessarily. Remember: Marriage, by definition, is the union between *two sexually different persons*. If this is true, then Gina and Kayla were never actually married in God's eyes and therefore won't be getting a divorce in God's eyes. They'd just be ending a sexual relationship out of allegiance to Christ.

- A church could make an accommodation for Gina and Kayla in the same way that it might accommodate a person who divorced his spouse for unbiblical reasons, got remarried, and now wants to join your church. This has become so commonplace today that perhaps we've forgotten that we're actually making an accommodation when we allow such divorced-and-remarried couples to join our churches.

- Some high-buffer churches might not allow Gina and Kayla to become members but would be willing to allow them to serve. (Many churches allow nonmembers to serve.) Some might be reluctant to have Gina serving on the worship team, since, you could argue, participating in the worship team presupposes that you're living a life of worship (i.e., obedience). Churches would probably be more eager to have Kayla serve in the outreach ministry, since this would be less of a leadership or "up front" role.

These are just some of the options available to high-buffer churches who don't see this as a secondary issue. Remember—consistency is the key. Churches should have the same standard for both straight and gay people.

You probably won't be surprised to hear that Gina and Kayla are actual people and that this scenario really happened. So what did the church do? Well, they allowed Kayla to serve in the outreach ministry, but because they considered worship to be in a different category, they didn't allow Gina to serve on the worship team. *However*—and this is where it gets really awesome—they told Gina that they would love to put on a Saturday night concert where Gina could share her amazing gifts with the church. Gina was a bit turned off by not being allowed to serve on the worship team, but after the church eagerly invited her to put on a concert, she knew that the church wasn't rejecting her, but was simply trying to maintain integrity toward their church's policy. But their no was quickly followed by a yes—a yes to Gina, and a yes to her gifts. *Gina—we want you here, we want you to belong, and we want you to bless others with the gifts God has given you!*

Whatever your church policy, whatever your situation, whatever your denomination, and whoever God brings your way, keep the supremacy of God and the gospel at the heart of everything you do. God is the one who saves, and God is the one who sanctifies. God reigns over church policies and works in and through the messes we sometimes create. This doesn't give us license to have sloppy and inconsistent church policies, and it shouldn't encourage us to let go and let God figure it all out. But it does mean that we should trust God to do the impossible, to break down the walls of hard hearts and conquer people with his love—a love that is free and yet costs us our life.

QUESTIONS FOR DISCUSSION

1. Discuss with the group your personal response to Gina and Kayla. Please give reasons for your approach and identify points of agreement and disagreement with the three bullet-pointed responses on pages 166–68.

2. If Gina and Kayla had a child in their care, would this change your response to their situation?

3. What are some things you would consider to be *primary* issues for your church? What are some things you would consider to be *secondary* issues?

4. Which type of membership policy—high buffer or low buffer—do you think is more faithful to Scripture, and why?

5. I say in this chapter, "We're living in a distinct cultural moment where there's much confusion about Christian sexual ethics." What are some of the other areas of sexual ethics about which some Christians may be confused in this "distinct cultural moment"? What are some about which there seems to be little confusion?

6. If an openly gay member of your church who's committed to celibacy and believes in a historically Christian view of marriage and sexuality wanted to be an elder, do you think he would be qualified? (Assuming, of course, that he meets the biblical qualifications of eldership.)

7. A lesbian couple attends your church. One of them is considering changing her sex from female to male. Assuming she goes through with the transition and then marries her fiancé, would that couple (now male/female—in their eyes and those who do not know them well) be able to become members of your church? Can they serve on the worship team? Can they serve on the elder team?

8. An elderly couple, both widowed, live together as if they are married, but without benefit of marriage because marriage negatively impacts their much-needed social security income. Both are lifelong members/family in the church. Everyone knows about the situation, but no one says anything because, well, these two are in their eighties and it's just embarrassing to discuss the possibilities of their sex life. The woman is nominated for an elected leadership/influence role. How might a high-buffer church and a low-buffer church address these two lovers?

9. Howard is a sixty-year-old elder at your church. He has faithfully served as an elder for twenty-two years and has taught several different Bible studies and been a pillar of godliness in the church. His grandson has recently come out as gay, which has prompted Howard to reexamine the issue of same-sex marriage. After studying the topic for the past six months, he has recently changed his view and now he's affirming of same-sex marriage. Even though the church holds to a historical view of marriage, Howard loves the church and still wants to stay at the church and remain on the elder board. He's not trying to convince people of his view, and yet he's still very honest with what he now believes and is eager to share his opinion if someone asks. Would you want Howard to remain an elder at your church?

10. In the video portion of this conversation, you watched Drew Harper tell a story about being invited to sing in the choir at a church. Drew is not a Christian, and yet he was clearly "so stoked!" (as he put it) to be wanted at the church. Would you be okay if Drew sang in the choir or in the worship team at your church? Why or why not?

ENDNOTES

1 Polygamy is of course a departure from the one-man, one-woman design of marriage. However, even in polygamous relationships, sex difference was still essential. Polygamous relationships were between one man and more than one woman, but not between the women in the marriage. (At least, there wasn't supposed to be anything going on between the women.)

2 See William Tucker, *Marriage and Civilization: How Monogamy Made Us Human* (Washington DC: Regnery, 2014).

Epilogue

Now that you've completed *Grace/Truth 1.0* and *2.0*, what are you going to do with the things you've learned? Consider these ideas:

1. Invite one of the leaders of your church to come to your group to discuss what is being done by the church to cultivate both grace and truth for LGBT+ people and their families.

2. Consider taking a group of your friends from other churches through *Grace/Truth 1.0*, if they haven't done so already.

3. Make a personal commitment to reach out to an LGBT+ person you know, or their family, in the next month. (It would be wonderful if your group heard a report of your experience.)

4. Pray about being an encourager to people wrestling with their faith, sexuality, or gender identity in your church. Include them in your life. Invite them into your family.

5. Reach out to people with LGBT+ relatives and listen to their stories. Sometimes families of LGBT+ kids or relatives get lost in the discussion (and debate). Make them feel loved and included.

6. If you have children who are old enough for this conversation, tell them what you've learned. Assure them that you will be a "safe person" if they ever need to talk about these issues.

As always, keep pursing both grace and truth in conversations about faith, sexuality, and gender. Grace without truth isn't grace; truth without grace isn't truth. We need both. We need to be passionate about both. One without the other isn't faithful to Christ. Balancing grace and truth, including them both, replicates and glorifies the presence of Jesus on earth.

THE CENTER FOR
FAITH, SEXUALITY & GENDER

The Center for Faith, Sexuality & Gender (The Center) is a collaboration of Christian pastors, leaders, and theologians who aspire to be the church's most trusted source of theologically sound teaching and practical guidance on questions related to sexuality and gender. The Center focuses on equipping Christian leaders, churches, and organizations to engage questions about faith, sexuality, and gender with theological faithfulness and courageous love.

At the Center, we seek to address two primary needs in the church. First, to help leaders cultivate a more robust biblical ethic of marriage, sexuality, and gender. Second, to help churches and organizations create a safe and compassionate environment for LGBT+ people, their families, and anyone wrestling with their sexuality or gender identity.

To meet these two needs, we seek not only to educate pastors and leaders but also to help these leaders educate the people they lead by providing small group material, educational videos, podcasts, blogs, youth curriculum, and other resources.

For more information, please visit www.centerforfaith.com.

Preston Sprinkle (PhD), president of
The Center for Faith, Sexuality & Gender